RAILWAYS OF BRITAIN

Kent and Sussex

Colin and David McCarthy

CONTENTS

Previous page: On the last day of passenger services on the Polegate-Hailsham section of the 'Cuckoo Line', as the Polegate-Eridge section was nicknamed, DEMU No 1112 awaits departure from Hailsham to Polegate with the 11.49am service on 8 September 1968. *John Vaughan*

First published 2007

ISBN (10) 0 7110 3222 X
ISBN (13) 978 0 7110 3222 4

Series Editor: Peter Waller

Published by Ian Allan Publishing

an imprint of Ian Allan Publishing Ltd, Hersham, Surrey KT12 4RG.

Printed by Ian Allan Printing Ltd, Hersham, Surrey KT12 4RG.

Visit the Ian Allan Publishing website at
www.ianallanpublishing.com

Code: 0710/C1

INTRODUCTION

In 2003, Colonel Michael Cobb published his superb two-volume atlas covering the railways of Great Britain. This work, widely praised when first published and subsequently reprinted and then reissued as a revised second edition, forms the basis of the cartography in this title in a series that is designed to provide a comprehensive historical guide to the railways of the country.

The cartography shows the railway infrastructure of the counties concerned. Alongside the railways, the major roads of the area are also shown so that readers can identify the inter-relationship between road and rail transport.

When compiling his original books, Michael Cobb decided to exclude those lines that were not constructed by the main line companies; these tended to be predominantly industrial lines; the intention here is to incorporate as many of these lines as possible. Unlike other areas, Kent and Sussex, being largely agrarian, lacked the large numbers of industrial railways that were a feature of areas such as the Lancashire coalfield; there were, however, a number, such as the Sittingbourne & Kemsley, and these are covered within the book's pages. Also included is an indication of locomotive sheds; fuller details of each of the sheds featured can be found in the book's narrative.

Supplementing the cartography, the book also includes an outline history of the lines featured together with a representative selection of photographs portraying the railway locations discussed. The book concludes with a full gazetteer of all the stations featured, giving opening and closing dates, as well as information about renaming if appropriate.

Notes on the maps

The maps are based upon the original work undertaken by Colonel Michael Cobb for his atlas; individual symbols are described within the key. The railway routes shown are differentiated between the lines that are open to passenger services, those that are open to freight traffic only, preserved lines and those closed completely. Station names with earlier versions are given; fuller details of the opening and closing dates of the stations can be found in the comprehensive index and gazetteer included at the back of the book. The major road network is shown as a means of placing the open and closed lines into their local context; the book, however, is not a road atlas and therefore minor roads are excluded.

OVERVIEW

The history of the railway development in the counties of Kent and Sussex is effectively an account of how three railway companies – the London, Brighton & South Coast; the London, Chatham & Dover; and the South Eastern – all endeavoured to dominate the provision of railway travel in this potentially highly profitable and prosperous part of Britain. The LBSCR came to have a virtually unassailable position in Sussex but in Kent there was considerable rivalry between the LC&DR and the SER that led to the construction of competing lines. It was not until 1899 and the creation of the South Eastern & Chatham that this bitter rivalry ceased. Apart from the LBSCR and the LC&DR/SER, there were also a number of minor lines constructed; in many of these the role of Colonel Holman F. Stephens was significant.

With the Canterbury & Whitstable and the London & Brighton, the area could lay claim to two of the earlier railway lines constructed in the country. The former was designed to provide a link between Canterbury and the port at Whitstable at a time when water remained the most effective means of moving freight, and the proximity of the sea to both counties was to have a profound impact on the region's railway development – from the Royal Navy's bases at Chatham and Portsmouth, to the cross-Channel ports at Newhaven, Folkestone, Dover and Ramsgate through to the boom in seaside holidays from the 1850s onwards. The most recent railway development in the area can be explained precisely because of this inter-relationship: the construction of the Channel Tunnel and of the Channel Tunnel Rail Link.

The counties of Kent and Sussex are predominantly rural with agriculture dominating much of the local economy, a fact emphasised by Kent's nickname as 'the Garden of England' and many of the lines were typical of rural branches and secondary routes constructed throughout the realm. There was, however, increasingly heavy industry, particularly in Kent and along the coast in Sussex. The discovery of the Kent coalfield resulted in some of the final lines to be constructed in the area, whilst other industries – such as papermaking and cement – also resulted in a number of industrial lines being constructed.

Whilst both Kent and Sussex might have been considered relatively remote at the dawn of the railway age by the late 20th century, as London became an ever more dominant factor in the southeast's economy, so travel patterns changed, with commuter services coming increasingly to dominate. Although there have been casualties amongst the region's lines – most notably in mid and south Sussex – the region did escape relatively lightly from the massive closures of the 1960s and early 1970s, with much of the network inherited by BR in 1948 still operational.

Apart from the remaining National Network routes, Kent and Sussex also possesses no fewer than five preserved lines that utilise closed BR lines as well as a number of other leisure railways, including the 'World's Smallest Public Railway' – the Romney, Hythe & Dymchurch.

HISTORY

Bognor Railway

Backed by the London, Brighton & South Coast Railway, the Bognor Railway was authorised on 11 July 1861 to construct a single-track line from Barnham Junction to the town. The line, operated by the LBSCR, opened on 1 June 1864 and the Bognor Railway was formally absorbed by the LBSCR on 29 July 1864. The station was rebuilt in 1902 and the branch was doubled in 1911. The branch was electrified as part of the Portsmouth No 2 project, inaugurated on 3 July 1938. The line remains open.

Left: The exterior of Bognor Regis station recorded in 1947. The station building dates to reconstruction in 1902. *Ian Allan Library*

Brighton & Chichester Railway

Incorporated by an Act of 4 July 1844, the line opened from Brighton to Worthing and thence to the original station called Littlehampton – not the branch terminus of that name – on 16 March 1846 and to Chichester on 8 June 1846. Effectively part of the London & Brighton Railway, the route became part of the London, Brighton & South Coast Railway following the creation of the larger company as a result of the Act of 27 July 1846. Prior to this, however, an extension to Portsmouth was authorised on 8 August 1845 and opened on 14 July 1847. The section between Chichester and Portsmouth was a joint line with the London & South Western Railway. The line was electrified between Brighton and West Worthing from 1 January 1933 and from West Worthing to Chichester on 3 July 1938. The line remains open throughout.

Below: Lancing station viewed in the Brighton direction on 28 April 1972. *John Scrace*

Right: On 30 April 1971 Class 2HAL No 2627 leads two 2-car units forming the 11.36 service from Littlehampton to Brighton at Worthing. *John Scrace*

Left: On 30 April 1971, '2BIL' No 2132 leads a pair of 2-car sets at Angmering with the 12.08 service from Portsmouth Harbour to Brighton. *John Scrace*

Right: The first station at Chichester opened on 8 June 1846 with the completion of the line from Brighton but the station was relocated to the west with the opening of the extension to Havant on 15 March 1847. The line through the station was electrified on 3 July 1938 and this photograph, taken the preceding month, records work in progress extending the platforms. Chichester station was progressively reconstructed between 1938 and the early 1960s. *Ian Allan Library*

Brighton & Dyke

This 3.5-mile long branch was authorised on 2 August 1877 and opened on 1 September 1887. Independent until the Grouping, the line was worked by the LBSCR although services were suspended between 1 January 1917 and 26 July 1920 as a result of World War 1. In 1910 the service comprised eight workings each weekday with five on Sundays. The journey time from The Dyke to Brighton was around 20 min. Taken over by the Southern Railway in 1923, freight services were withdrawn on 2 January 1933 and passenger services on 1 January 1939. Devil's Dyke, where the branch terminated, was a popular tourist destination. The line climbed 400ft in its short distance with gradients of up to 1 in 40.

Below: With the junction signalbox in the background, 'Terrier' No 79 *Minories* waits at Dyke Junction with a motor train. Following the closure of The Dyke branch the station was subsequently rebuilt with concrete platforms and in June 1932 became Aldrington Halt.
Ian Allan Library

Brighton, Lewes & Hastings Railway

Authorised on 29 July 1844, the 32.5-mile long BL&HR was notionally independent but became part of the LBSCR on 27 July 1846. The line opened from Brighton to Lewes on 8 June 1846, to Bulverhythe on 27 June 1846 and to St Leonards on 7 November 1846. The final section, to Hastings, was opened on 13 February 1851. Powers to construct a six-mile branch from Lewes to Newhaven were obtained on 8 June 1846 but did not open until 8 December 1847 after the line had passed to the LBSCR. The line from Brighton to Hastings was electrified on 7 July 1935 and remains open today. The Newhaven line, subsequently extended to Seaford, was electrified on 7 July 1935. Services are provided by the Southern franchise.

Right: The first station east of Brighton on the line towards Lewes is London Road. The station was officially renamed London Road (Brighton) at Grouping, although this change of name is not reflected in this view. *Lens of Sutton*

Left: The 11.2am service from Brighton to London Victoria arrives at Lewes on 26 March 1955 behind 2-6-4T No 42104. *Pamlin Prints*

Right: Class 4COR No 3102 departs from Lewes with the 15.11 service from Ore to Brighton on 28 April 1972. *John Scrace*

Left: Newhaven Harbour station opened originally on 17 May 1886. It is recorded here on 5 April 1983.
John Scrace

Right: On 26 July 1963, 'A1X' No 32678 is recorded heading across the Newhaven swing bridge light engine for West Quay.
E. Wilmshurst

Left: Continental station, Newhaven Harbour, viewed on 12 September 1967 from the footbridge of Newhaven Harbour station, the platform of which can be seen in the left foreground. The French-owned car ferry *Villandry* stands alongside the quay.
H. A. Gamble

Brighton, Uckfield & Tunbridge Wells Railway

Authorised on 22 July 1861, the 15.5-mile long BU&TWR was opened from Uckfield to Groombridge, where it met the East Grinstead, Groombridge & Tunbridge Wells Railway, and thence to Tunbridge Wells to freight in 1867 and to passenger traffic on 3 August 1868. The station at Uckfield was relocated slightly to the north on 13 May 1991. The section of line from Birchden Junction to Groombridge and Tunbridge Wells lost its passenger services on 8 July 1985 and was closed completely on 12 August 1985. The line from Eridge to Tunbridge Wells West now forms part of the preserved Spa Valley Railway.

Below: Eridge station viewed looking towards the south in 1947. The line remains open through Eridge to serve Uckfield. *Ian Allan Library*

Right: Viewed looking towards the east, Groombridge station is recorded in 1948. Passenger services over the line to Tunbridge Wells West were withdrawn on 8 July 1985 and much of the station site at Groombridge has been redeveloped for housing, although the preserved Spa Valley Railway operates through the site. *Ian Allan Library*

Left: Recorded on 25 May 1958, this view taken looking towards the west shows to good effect the scale of the facilities at Tunbridge Wells West. Following closure of the line in 1985, BR moved quickly to sever the connection with Tunbridge Wells Central. Today, the station building survives in commercial use.
J. Scrace

Right: The original station at Uckfield viewed looking towards the southwest sees Class 207 DEMU No 1311 having arrived with the 11.13 service from Victoria. The station was to be relocated 50m to the north, across the level crossing, in 1991.
Brian Morrison

Above: On 13 July 1985 DEMU No 1311 awaits departure from Buxted with the 13.24 service from Victoria to Uckfield. *John Scrace*

Canterbury & Whitstable

One of the oldest railways in the United Kingdom and the first in southern England to be operated by steam – the original line's only locomotive built by Robert Stephenson *Invicta* is now preserved – the C&WR was authorised on 10 June 1825 and built by Joseph Locke. The six-mile long line opened on 3 May 1830 with an extension to Whitstable Harbour following on 19 March 1832. The line included the 1,012yd long tunnel under Tyler Hill and was also steeply graded – with one section of 836yd hitting 1 in 31. *Invicta* was not successful with the result that it was replaced by stationary engines; these lasted until operation of the line was taken over by the SER on 29 September 1844. Passenger services ceased on 1 January 1931 and freight followed on 1 December 1952, although there was a short reprieve in early 1953 following severe flooding. Final closure came on 2 March 1953.

Channel Tunnel

Proposals for the construction of a Channel Tunnel between Britain and France date back to the 19th century but it was not until the 1970s that the first serious effort to undertake construction was started. However, the work ceased on this project in 1975, when the Labour government led by Harold Wilson withdrew funding. The project lay dormant until the early 1980s when the scheme was revived but based around private rather than public investment. Work commenced under the auspices of Eurotunnel with work being undertaken by Trans Manche Link in 1987. The historic breakthrough ceremony occurred on 1 December 1990 and the tunnel was officially opened on 6 May 1994. Eurostar services were introduced between London and Paris or Brussels on 14 November 1994 and the shuttle services on 22 December 1994.

Channel Tunnel Rail Link

Although the Channel Tunnel itself was opened at the end of 1994 and fast links were completed in France by the opening date and through to Brussels three years later, proposals for a similar fast link in Britain were to develop later and were beset with funding problems initially. In 1996 London & Continental Railways was selected to build and operate the Channel Tunnel Rail Link although the operational rights were subsequently transferred to Network Rail (who will also manage and maintain the line). The first phase of the CTRL opened from the Tunnel itself, via a reopened section of the Fawkham Junction-Gravesend West line, in September 2003 with the remainder, through a new station at Ebbsfleet International, opening on 14 November 2007. This will result in the cessation of Eurostar services operating over Network Rail lines into Waterloo station.

Chattenden Naval Tramway

Constructed by the Admiralty following a Light Railway Order of 24 July 1901, the CNT was a two-mile long standard gauge line that connected Lodge Hill eastwards to Sharnal Street. A second line, authorised before the war but not opened until 1915, ran eastwards from Sharnal Street to Kingsnorth. The latter section was taken over by the Kingsnorth Light Railway in the 1920s, with the line ultimately closing in 1940. The original CNT closed in 1961.

Chattenden & Upnor Railway

Pre-dating the CNT was the Chattenden & Upnor Railway, which ran south from Lodge Hill to Upnor. Originally built as a standard gauge line in the 1870s, the line was converted to 2ft 6in by the Royal Engineers in the 1890s before being transferred to the Admiralty on 1 April 1906. The line was to survive two World Wars before being finally closed on 31 December 1961.

Chichester & Midhurst Railway

Authorised to construct a 12-mile long branch from Chichester to Midhurst on 23 June 1864, the company collapsed before the line could be completed and the powers passed to the LBSCR on 13 July 1876. The line was opened on 11 July 1881. Passenger services over the line were withdrawn on 7 July 1935 with the line remaining open to freight thereafter. In 1910 there were six workings on weekdays from Midhurst to Chichester and a seventh from Singleton to Chichester, with seven in the reverse direction. There was no service on Sundays. The journey time, calling at all stations, was about 35min. The section of line between Cocking and Midhurst was closed as a result of flooding on 20 November 1951. The section between Cocking and Lavant closed completely on 31 August 1953 and that from the junction at Chichester to Lavant, retained for ballast and beet traffic, finally closed completely on 15 March 1991.

Cranbrook & Paddock Wood Railway

Initially incorporated on 2 August 1877 and with an extension to Hawkhurst authorised on 12 July 1882, the powers lapsed as a result of financial problems the powers lapsed until they were resurrected by the SER by an Act of 12 July

Right: There were three intermediate stations between Midhurst and Chichester; the northernmost of the trio was Cocking. Although undated, the photograph can be dated to the brief period between November 1951 and August 1953 when Cocking was the terminus of the freight-only service from Chichester. The line north of Cocking had been severed late in 1951 as a result of flooding. *Ian Allan Library*

Below: Goudhurst – originally called Hope Mill when first opened – was one of three intermediate stations that once served the Hawkhurst branch. Here 'C' class No 31717 and 'D' class No 31729 double-head a hop-pickers' special back from Hawkhurst to London Bridge at the station on a late September evening in the early 1950s. *K. G. Carr*

1887. The line opened to Hope Mill – called Goudhurst from December 1892 – on 1 October 1892 and throughout on 4 September 1893. Operated by the SER from the start, the C&PWR was absorbed by the larger company on 10 June 1900. In 1910 there were 10 return workings each weekday with two on Sundays. Calling at all intermediate stations, the journey time over the 11.5-mile long branch was just under 30min. Passenger services were withdrawn, and the line closed completely, on 12 June 1961.

Left: Pictured less than a month before total closure, the branch terminus at Hawkhurst is recorded here looking in the up direction from the buffer stops on 27 May 1961.
John Scrace

Right: Cranbrook was the penultimate station on the Hawkhurst branch. Opened on 4 September 1893, the station is viewed here on 22 July 1933. The noticeboard proudly proclaims its pre-Grouping origins, referring to the South Eastern & Chatham Railway Companies Managing Committee.
H. C. Casserley

Crowhurst, Sidley & Bexhill Railway

Authorised on 15 July 1897 and opened, operated by the SER from the outset, on 1 June 1902, the CS&BR became part of the SER on 1 January 1907 following an Act of 4 August 1906. The popularity of Bexhill had increased as a result of it being the first British resort to permit mixed bathing. In 1910 there were eight return workings per day with six on Sundays. The journey time over the 4.5-mile long branch was about 10min. Services over the line were suspended between 1 January 1917 and 1 March 1919 as a result of World War 1. Freight services over the branch ceased on 9 September 1963 and the line closed completely with the withdrawal of passenger services on 15 June 1964.

Right: The Bexhill West branch possessed one intermediate station – Sidley – viewed here looking towards the Crowhurst direction in 1951. *Ian Allan Library*

Left: Bexhill West was the SECR's terminus in the town following the branch's opening on 1 June 1902. The spacious terminus, designed to cope with the hordes travelling to and from the town during the holiday season, is recorded in this view looking towards the south in 1931. The branch was to survive until the Beeching era, when it became one of the relatively few lines in the area to be threatened with closure. The line was to close completely on 15 June 1964. *Ian Allan Library*

Dover & Deal Joint Railway

The only joint line constructed by the LC&DR and SER before the two companies set up the joint management committee, the 8.5-mile long line was authorised to run from Buckland Junction, north of Dover, to Deal. Incorporated on 30 June 1874, work commenced on 29 June 1878 and the line opened on 15 June 1881. Electrified as part of the Kent Coast scheme, the route saw electric services introduced on 18 June 1962 and the line remains operational today with the exception of the curve from Deal Junction to Kearsney Loop Junction, which closed completely on 8 August 1971.

Dover & Martin Mill Light Railway

In order to assist in the construction of the harbour at Dover, the contractors built a line south from Martin Mill. After the construction was completed in 1909 there were proposals to convert the line into a passenger-carrying route, but these did not proceed and the line was lifted.

Left: On 20 September 1958 'L1' class 4-4-0 No 31754 heads the 9.38am service from Chatham to Dover as it passes Deal Junction signalbox at Kearsney. The section of line from Deal Junction box to Kearsney Loop Junction — visible passing behind the box — closed completely in 1971. *J. H. Aston*

East Grinstead Railway

Authorised on 8 July 1853, the EGR was empowered to construct a line from Three Bridges to East Grinstead. Work commenced on constructing the line on 22 November 1853 and the line opened on 9 July 1855. Worked by the LBSCR, the larger company was empowered to take over the smaller company on 28 June 1858, doing so on 1 January 1865. Passenger services over the line were withdrawn on 2 January 1967 at which time the line was to close completely.

Below: Rowfant was one of two intermediate stations on the line between Three Bridges and East Grinstead. On 6 August 1956 Class M7 0-4-4T No 30052 makes a brief call at the station with the 4.49pm service from Three Bridges to East Grinstead. *G. Daniels*

Above: A dramatic view that illustrates well the relationship between the High and Low Level stations in East Grinstead. On 2 March 1963 'H' class 0-4-4T No 31518 propels the 1.27pm push-pull service to Three Bridges out of the High Level station. At Low Level, the tracks can be seen heading off towards St Margaret's Junction and the connection between the two stations.
G. D. King

East Grinstead, Groombridge & Tunbridge Wells Railway

Incorporated on 7 August 1862, the company was authorised to construct a line from East Grinstead to Groombridge, where a connection was made with the Brighton, Uckfield & Tunbridge Wells Railway. The line was taken over by the LBSCR on 29 July 1864 and opened on 1 October 1866. Passenger services over the line were withdrawn on 2 January 1967, at which time the sections from Ashurst West Junction to East Grinstead and the connecting line at East Grinstead between the High and Low Level stations was to close completely.

East Kent Railway

Authorised on 4 August 1853, the EKR was empowered to construct a 48.5-mile long line from Strood to Canterbury and to use the SER's station at Strood. The EKR was also empowered to construct a short branch at Faversham to the Quay and a link to the SER at Chilham. The Chatham-Faversham line opened on 25 January 1858 and, with a bridge across the Medway, was extended from Chatham to Strood on 29 March 1858. The Faversham Quay line opened on 12 April 1860; the link to Chilham was never completed. On 30 July 1855 further powers were obtained to extend the line from Canterbury to Dover. In its early years the EKR – or London, Chatham & Dover as it became on 1 August 1859 – was beset by financial problems. Thus the line from Faversham to Canterbury, which opened on 3 July 1860, was originally constructed as single track. The extension from Canterbury to Dover opened on 22 July 1861. The line through from Swanley Junction to Gillingham was electrified with services commencing on 2 July 1939. From Gillingham to Dover the route was electrified from 15 June 1959. Apart from the Faversham Quay line, closed in the 1980s, the entire route from Strood to Dover remains open with contemporary services provided by the South Eastern franchise. In 1858, following the refusal of the SER to grant running powers over its line from Strood towards London, the East Kent obtained powers to construct its own route from Rochester to connect with the Mid-Kent line at St Mary Cray. This line opened on 3 December 1860 and provided the new LC&DR with its own main line from London to the Channel.

Below: The station at Rochester, seen here looking towards the west in 1914, was relocated to the current site on 1 March 1892 and rebuilt in 1911. *Ian Allan Library*

Left: It's February 1957 and work is in progress with the first phase of the Kent Coast electrification scheme. Amongst the work required was the extension of the platforms at Rainham as recorded in this view. Electric services over this section of the former LC&DR route would commence in the summer of 1959. *Ian Allan Library*

Right: Chatham was a naval base until closure in the early 1980s and was linked to the railway network via a short branch that connected at Gillingham. On 3 March 1968 the LCGB 'Invicta' tour visited the line; the train was headed by Class 08 shunter D3465 with Class 33 No D6566 at the rear. *Stephen May*

Left: On 12 June 1976, the 16.14 Ramsgate-Victoria fast service, formed of class 423 No 7872 and Class 411/2 No 7175, arrives at Faversham. *A. W. Hobson*

Right: Selling station, the only intermediate station between Faversham and Canterbury East, opened five months after the line on 3 December 1860. This view shows the main station buildings on the up platform on 22 September 1975. *John Scrace*

Left: Opened on 9 July 1860, Canterbury East was the terminus of the line from Faversham until the completion of the line to Dover. This view, taken looking towards the northwest, shows the station when still complete with its overall roof.
Ian Allan Library

Right: Shepherd's Well was the junction for the East Kent Light Railway, the junction to which was located slightly to the north of the station. On 6 May 1960, the 1.40pm coal train from Shepherd's Well to Dover departs from the station behind 'O1' class No 31258.
Derek Cross

Left: The next station from Shepherd's Well towards Dover was Stonehall & Lydden Halt. Here 'L1' class 4-4-0 No 31753 heads south with a Sunday service from Faversham to Dover; this train was non-stop through this station. The station was destined to close on 5 April 1954.
W. A. Corkill

Right: Dover Priory was originally known as Dover Town (Priory) when first opened, being named after the adjacent St Martin's Priory. It was a terminus station for a brief period from opening on 22 July 1861 until the completion of the extension to Dover Harbour on 1 November 1861. This is the view through the short Priory Tunnel to the north of the station on 3 September 1968 and shows the signalbox at north end of the platform.
John Scrace

Left: The original Dover Harbour station opened on 1 November 1861 with the extension of the line from Dover Priory. This was closed in 1863 and replaced by a new station, Dover Town & Harbour, which was itself renamed Dover Harbour on 1 July 1899. This is the station recorded in this 1925 view. The station was to be closed two years later on 10 July 1927.
Ian Allan Library

Right: Originally known as Sevenoaks Junction when first opened on 1 July 1862, the station was renamed Swanley Junction in 1871. The original station was closed in 1939 as part of the electrification scheme although the remains of the original station remain visible in the 'V' of the junction. This was the view of the original station, looking in the down direction, in 1948.
Ian Allan Library

Left: This view, taken in July 1939, shows the newly completed replacement station at Swanley Junction constructed slightly to the west of the original station as part of the scheme for the electrification of the line to Sevenoaks. *Ian Allan Library*

East Kent Light Railway

The discovery of a coalfield along the Kent coast provided a spur to the development of another of the area's independent railways – the East Kent Light Railway. The line, engineered by Holman Stephens, was authorised by a Light Railway Order dated 19 June 1911. The line commenced freight traffic in November 1912 but it was not until 16 October 1916 that passenger services were introduced on the 10.25-mile long section from Shepherd's Well to Wingham. The company had plans to extend to Canterbury but got no further

Below: The EKR's Shepherd's Well station viewed looking towards the buffer stops in 1933. *Ian Allan Library*

than Canterbury Road – the extension from Wingham opening in 1925 – with the line from Eastry to Richborough via Sandwich Road also opening in 1925. Although stations were built to serve the section north of Sandwich Road to Richborough, these were never used and passenger services from Eastry to Sandwich Road themselves lasted only until 31 October 1928. The EKR passed to BR in 1948 and, on 30 October 1948, passenger services between Shepherd's Well and Canterbury Road were withdrawn. The line between Eastry and Richborough closed completely on 27 October 1949. This was followed by the closure of the section from Eastry to Canterbury Road on 25 July 1950 and that between Eythorne and Eastry on 1 July 1951. The remaining section – from Shepherd's Well to Tilmanstone Colliery – survived until 1 March 1984. The remaining section now forms the basis of the preserved East Kent Railway, formed in 1985 to preserve the remaining section of the line.

Elham Valley Railway

Construction of the 16.25-mile long EVR was authorised on 18 July 1885 but, before the line was opened, it was taken over, following an Act of 28 July 1884, by the SER. The line opened from Shorncliffe (Cheriton Junction) to Barham on 4 July 1887 and thence to Canterbury (Harbledown Junction) on 1 July 1889. Initially constructed as double track, the route was singled during World War I. The line was effectively worked as part of a circular service linking Folkestone, Canterbury and Minster. In 1910 there were seven return workings per weekday with an additional service on Thursdays from Folkestone to Barham. There were four return workings on Sundays. Passenger services were withdrawn between Lyminge and Canterbury on 2 December 1940 with the remaining section operating for the army alone until services were withdrawn on 3 May 1943. Passenger services from Lyminge to Shorncliffe were reintroduced on 7 October 1946 before being finally withdrawn on 16 June 1947. The line was to close completely on 10 October 1947.

Gravesend Railway

Incorporated on 18 July 1881, the GR was empowered to construct a four-mile line from Fawkham Junction to Gravesend with an extension, authorised on 24 July 1882, to West Street Pier, Gravesend. The double-track line, costing £650,000, was opened on 10 May 1886, having been taken over by the LC&DR on 29 June 1883. Passenger services were withdrawn between Fawkham and Gravesend West on 17 April 1953 and the section from Southfleet to Gravesend West was to close completely on 24 March 1968. The final section, from Fawkham to Southfleet, where there was a cement works, closed on 26 January 1976. The southernmost section of the line from Fawkham reopened in 2003 to provide a connection with the first phase of the Channel Tunnel Rail Link into the National Network, thereby allowing access to Eurostar services to and from Waterloo.

Gravesend & Rochester Railway

Promoted by the Thames & Medway Canal Co and authorised on 31 July 1845, this single-track railway linking Gravesend with Strood was opened on

Above: Gravesend West Street was the terminus of the branch from Fawkham Junction. The branch terminus is viewed here in 1948, some five years before passenger services were withdrawn. *Ian Allan Library*

10 February 1845. The line was initially constructed alongside the existing canal. However, following an Act of 3 August 1846, the line and canal were acquired by the SER for £310,000. The first line was closed in November 1846 to allow for the tunnel to be filled in and a double-track railway constructed. The line reopened on 23 August 1847. Using a ferry across the Medway, a through service from Rochester to London was introduced on 30 July 1849. The line from Strood to Gravesend was electrified as part of the final prewar electrification scheme, with services being introduced on 2 July 1939. Today, as part of the North Kent line, the route remains operational.

Herne Bay & Faversham Railway

Authorised on 17 August 1857, the company's name was changed to the Margate Railway in 1859 when powers to extend the line to Margate were obtained.

Horsham & Guildford Direct Railway

Authorised to construct a 15.5-mile single-track line from Horsham (Stammerham Junction) to Guildford (Peasmarsh Junction) via Cranleigh, the H&GDR was unfinished when taken over by the LBSCR following an Act of 29 July 1864. The line opened on 2 October 1865. Passenger services over the route were withdrawn on 14 June 1965, on which date the line closed completely.

Horsham, Dorking & Leatherhead Railway

Promoted by the LBSCR, only the southernmost section of this line, including one of the intermediate stations (Warnham), is in Sussex. The line itself was incorporated on 17 July 1862 and the section from Dorking to Horsham opened on 1 May 1867. The line was electrified as part of the Mid-Sussex scheme, with services commencing on 3 July 1938. The station at Horsham was rebuilt at the same time. Today, passenger services, now controlled by the Southern franchise, operate over the route.

Right: An Ivatt 2-6-2T, No 41294, departs from Christ's Hospital station, the junction for the line to Guildford, with the 10.34am service from Guildford on 26 September 1964.
John Scrace

Below: The first intermediate station north of the junction at Christ's Hospital was Slinfold. On 14 September 1963, less than two years before the line closed, Ivatt 2-6-2T No 41300 is pictured heading northbound with the 4.53pm service from Horsham.
J. H. Aston

Hundred of Hoo Railway

Authorised on 21 July 1879, the HHR was backed by the South Eastern Railway, which took it over on 11 August 1881. The 11-mile long single-track branch opened from Hoo Junction to Sharnal Street on 1 April 1882 and to Port Victoria, where construction of a pier was authorised on 2 August 1880, on 11 September 1882. Ferry services from the pier ceased in 1901 and the pier itself closed in 1916. In 1910 there were six return workings on Mondays, nine on Saturdays and three on Sundays. The journey time for a single journey to

Above: Heading north from Slinfold, the second of the four intermediate stations on the line was Rudgwick. The single platform, station building and signalbox at the station are shown to good effect in this view taken looking in the Guildford direction in 1948. *Ian Allan Library*

Left: SR No A311 pictured at Port Victoria Pier on 26 April 1930. *H. C. Casserley*

or from Gravesend was just under 40min. Passenger services over the section from Grain Crossing Halt to Port Victoria ceased on 4 September 1951 and those from Hoo Junction to the new station at Grain followed on 4 December 1961; however, industrial development in the Grain and Port Victoria areas has ensured that the line has remained open thereafter as a freight-only route.

Hundred of Man & Selsey Tramway

Opened on 27 August 1897 and built without parliamentary sanction, the standard-gauge Selsey tramway ran for 7.75 miles from Chichester, where the line had its own station, to Selsey. A short half-mile extension to Selsey Beach was opened on 1 August 1898; this operated in summer months only and was closed during World War 1 and never reopened. Apart from the two termini,

Right: The somewhat basic station at Port Victoria recorded in 1948 some three years before passenger services over the section from Grain to the station were withdrawn. *Ian Allan Library*

Right: On 9 July 1955, 'C' class No 31495 passes High Halstow Halt with the 3.50pm freight from All Hallows to Hoo Junction. In the foreground can be seen Wybourne Siding signalbox. *J. H. Aston*

there were six intermediate stations and two private halts (Hoe Farm and Golf Club). In 1927 there were seven return workings per weekday from Selsey to Chichester (eight on Mondays) with two return workings on Sundays. The single journey time was 30min. The line was one of a number under the control of Holman F. Stephens and, like others in his empire, the line used a variety of types of motive power, including petrol-driven railcars. In 1924 the company's legal position was regularised following an order granted under the Railway Construction Facilities Act, after which it was officially known as the West Sussex Light Railway. During the 1920s the company's financial position deteriorated and the line closed completely on 19 January 1935, although a limited number of trains – to clear stock and any remaining freight – ran during the following week. The line was lifted in 1936 and the company was officially wound up two years later.

Left: Built by Peckett in 1897, 2-4-2T *Selsey* is pictured departing from Chichester with a freight in 1921. This was one of two steam locomotives to survive until the final closure of the line in 1935 and was also the only locomotive to be acquired new from the builders. After closure the locomotive, deemed beyond economic repair, was scrapped.
Ian Allan Library

Left: Acquired in 1917, *Ringing Rock* was an 0-6-0ST originally constructed by Manning Wardle in 1883. It is seen here at Pagham Harbour, between Sidlesham and Ferry stations, with a typical mixed train. *Ringing Rock* was the second locomotive to survive until final closure.
Ian Allan Library

Industrial Lines

Although early in the railway age both Kent and Sussex were predominantly rural areas, both had had a tradition of industry, particularly along the coastal fringe and along the Thames estuary. Certain industries – coal after the discovery of the Kent coalfield at the end of the 19th century, cement and paper – came to dominate the local economy in places like Sittingbourne and in the Deal and Dover area. Much of the traffic to and from the factories was carried by rail and, in certain cases, extensive networks were constructed to serve the plants concerned. Of these the most significant was perhaps the narrow gauge network constructed by Bowaters to serve the paper mills in and around Sittingbourne. This 2ft 6in gauge network was originally opened in 1906 with steam traction being introduced two years later. By the date of the line's closure in 1969 it was the last steam-operated industrial narrow gauge line in Britain. Following closure a section was leased as the preserved Sittingbourne & Kemsley Light Railway.

Kent & East Sussex Light Railway

Following an order of 1904, the Rother Valley Railway became the Kent & East Sussex Light Railway on 1 June 1904. One of a number of lines managed by Colonel Holman Stephens, the extension from Tenterden to Headcorn opened on 15 May 1905. Despite the death of Stephens and financial problems, the K&ESR survived to pass to BR in 1948. Passenger services were withdrawn on 4 January 1954, at which time the extension north from Tenterden to Headcorn closed completely.

Right: The narrow gauge network constructed by Bowaters to serve the company's paper mills around Sittingbourne was Kent's most extensive network of narrow gauge lines and, following closure in 1969, a section was preserved by the LCGB as the Sittingbourne & Kemsley Light Railway. On 23 September 1969, shortly before the line closed, *Conqueror* was recorded at Kemsley having just arrived with a train from Ridham dock. *Alastair McIntyre*

Kent Coast Railway

Renamed from the Margate Railway, the KCR was authorised to extend its earlier line to Ramsgate. The line from Herne Bay to Ramsgate opened on 5 October 1863 and was operated from the outset by the LC&DR. The larger company absorbed the smaller KCR on 1 July 1871. The line terminated in a station located adjacent to the harbour; known as Ramsgate Harbour from

Left: On 12 August 1963, the 3.30pm mixed train to Headcorn prepares to depart from Tenterden Town station behind 'O1' class 0-6-0 No 31065.
Geoffrey F. Bannister

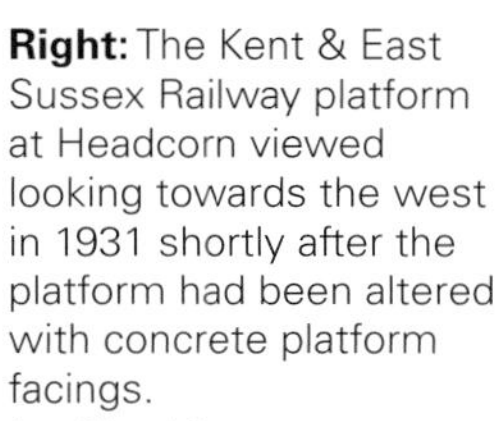

Right: The Kent & East Sussex Railway platform at Headcorn viewed looking towards the west in 1931 shortly after the platform had been altered with concrete platform facings.
Ian Allan Library

Left: Between Herne Bay and Ramsgate Harbour there were five intermediate stations. After Birchington-on-Sea there was Westgate-on-Sea, which opened in April 1871. This view of the station, taken looking towards the east, was recorded on 10 September 1968.
John Scrace

Right: Viewed looking towards the north in 1933 Broadstairs station opened with the line on 5 October 1863.
Ian Allan Library

1899, the station was to close on 2 July 1926 when the SR opened its link line via Dumpton Park. The remainder of the route was electrified as part of the first phase of the Kent Coast scheme on 15 June 1959. The line is now served by the South Eastern franchise.

Kingsnorth Light Railway

Constructed as a two-mile extension of the Chattenden Naval Tramway, following an agreement of 14 August 1924, the Kingsnorth Light Railway worked the line from 24 July 1926 and took over ownership following an order dated 25 July 1929. The line closed in 1940.

Right: The four-platform station known as Ramsgate Harbour after 1899 was approached through a 1,630yd-long tunnel and a 1 in 75 gradient. This view, taken from the carriage sidings in 1924 two years before the station closed, shows the tracks entering the tunnel on the right, the overall roof of the station in the centre and the locomotive servicing facility beneath the cliff.
Ian Allan Library

Lewes & East Grinstead Railway

Running from Crowhurst Junction, near Oxted, to Culver Junction, 3.75 miles north of Lewes on the line towards Eridge, and with a branch from Horsted Keynes to Copyhold Junction, just to the north of Haywards Heath, the L&EGR was authorised on 10 August 1877. Nominally independent when promoted, problems in raising the finance led to the LBSCR effectively taking the line over following an Act of 17 June 1878. The main line was opened on 1 August 1882 with the three-mile long Copyhold Junction branch following on 3 September 1883. Passenger services over the section south from East Grinstead were originally withdrawn on 28 May 1955; however, legal action followed as a result of a clause in the 1878 agreement that had guaranteed a certain level of service. As a result BR was forced to reintroduce a service on 7 August 1956, which continued to operate until new powers to close were obtained. Once permitted, BR again withdrew the passenger service, on 17 March 1958, at which time the section between East Grinstead and Culver Junction was closed completely. Passenger services over the section from Copyfold Junction to Horsted Keynes – electrified on 7 July 1935 – closed to passenger services on 28 October 1963 at which time the section from Ardingly to Horsted Keynes closed completely. The Ardingly section remains open to serve a quarry. The line north from East Grinstead, electrified in October 1987, remains operational, with services provided by the Southern franchise. The section from Sheffield Park to Kingscote is preserved as the Bluebell Railway, and the preservationists are rebuilding back towards East Grinstead. The section of closed line from Horsted Keynes to Ardingly is now also owned by the Bluebell Railway.

Lewes & Uckfield Railway

Incorporated on 27 July 1857, the line from Lewes to Uckfield was opened officially on 11 October 1858. Following authorisation on 1 August 1859, the LBSCR took over the company on 31 May 1860. Passenger trains over the route ceased on 23 February 1969 (at which date the line closed completely),

Left: Horsted Keynes recorded looking towards the north in 1953 sees Ivatt 2-6-2T No 41297 arriving at the station with a service from Oxted to Lewes. The third rail seen on the westernmost track is evidence of the electrified service from Haywards Heath. It was the presence of electric services, which operated until closure in 1963, that precluded the Bluebell Railway from operating into Horsted Keynes station when the section south to Sheffield Park was first preserved.
R. C. Riley/Transport Treasury

although bus replacement services continued until the date of official closure on 6 May 1969. A short section north of one of the intermediate stations – Isfield – has been preserved as the Lavender Line. The Lewes-Uckfield line is one of the long-closed lines for which there has been considerable pressure for reopening, particularly to provide an alternative route for the London-Brighton main line.

London & Brighton Railway

Authorised on 15 July 1837, the London & Brighton was empowered to construct a line from the London & Croydon route at Selhurst to the south coast. Work started on 12 July 1838 with the cutting of the first sod at Merstham Tunnel, with the first section of the 4ft 9in gauge line from Brighton to Shoreham opening on 12 May 1840 (this was constructed and opened first as materials for the remainder of the line could be landed at Shoreham Harbour). The section from Norwood Junction to Haywards Heath was opened on 12 July 1841 with the section thence to Brighton opening on 21 September. The line was engineered by John Urpeth Raistrick. Following mergers with the Brighton & Chichester, Brighton, Lewes & Hastings and London & Croydon railways in 1845 and 1846, the company's name changed to the London, Brighton & South Coast Railway. The London-Brighton main line was electrified in the early 1930s, with services reaching Three Bridges on 17 July 1932 and being extended officially south to Brighton on 31 December 1932. Public services to Brighton commenced on 1 January 1933, the same day as electric services were extended to run to West Worthing via Shoreham. Both routes remain open, with services being operated by a number of franchisees, including Southern and First Capital Connect.

London, Brighton & South Coast Railway

Formed by the merger of the London & Brighton and London & Croydon railways on 27 July 1846, the LBSCR was to become one of the three main constituents of the Southern Railway at the Grouping in 1923. The vast

Right: Three Bridges is the first intermediate station on the London-Brighton line in Sussex heading south. The station first opened on 12 July 1841, with certain of the structures on the down platform dating from David Mocatta's original work on the line. The station's importance grew with the opening of the lines towards Horsham and East Grinstead, although the latter is now closed. This view was taken on 18 April 1976, looking towards the north. *John Scrace*

Left: Balcombe station is situated just to the south of the 1,141yd long Balcombe Tunnel and dates to the opening of the line on 12 July 1841. The tunnel was the location of a notorious murder in 1881 when a passenger on a down train was thrown from a carriage window; the perpetrator was caught eventually at Preston Park station and was subsequently tried and executed for his crime. Here, on a more peaceful occasion (30 May 1968), DEMU No 1203 is recorded at Balcombe.
John Scrace

Left: Preston Park station opened as Preston on 1 November 1869. The station is viewed here on 30 June 1977.
John Scrace

Left: On 11 April 1964 Ivatt 2-6-2T No 41303 waits to depart from Brighton with the 11.37am service to Horsham. The main station buildings were the work of David Mocatta, the architect employed by the London & Brighton Railway, and are amongst the significant buildings to survive from his work for the railway.
G. D. King

Right: LBSCR 4-6-4T No 329 *Stephenson* heads southbound through Hassocks station with a service to Brighton. The station opened as Hassocks Gate on 21 September 1841, being renamed some 40 years later. Situated midway up the 1 in 264 gradient to the summit of the section through the South Downs beyond Clayton Tunnel, Hassocks was the station used for excursion traffic to the Downs. *Ian Allan Library*

Left: The view north from Brighton station on 8 July 1979 sees the 15.10 service for London Victoria having just departed. In the foreground can be seen a number of Classes 33 and 73 stabled along with stores EMU No 023 (converted from a '2HAL' unit in 1970). The background is dominated by the 400yd-long viaduct on the line towards Lewes; the viaduct and line east from Brighton opened on 8 June 1846. *Les Bertram*

Right: The first section of the London & Brighton Railway to be completed was the section from Brighton to Shoreham, which opened on 12 May 1840. The original Hove station was located about half a mile closer to Brighton than the present station, which was opened originally as Cliftonville on 1 October 1865. This view, taken looking towards the west on 8 July 1979, sees '4VEP' No 7880 leaving Hove station with the 12.01 service from Littlehampton to Brighton. *Les Bertram*

majority of the lines that the LBSCR passed to the SR were constructed under the auspices of separate or earlier companies and the history of these lines is outlined under the names of the companies that promoted the routes concerned. There were, however, a number of lines directly promoted by the LBSCR. These included:

- Keymer Junction-Lewes – This line opened on 1 October 1847. A station at Keymer Junction, with platforms only on the Lewes line, opened in 1854; the original station closed on 1 January 1862 to be replaced by a second station in the same location. This itself closed 20 years later to be replaced with a station north of the junction, which was renamed Wivelsfield in 1896. Further intermediate stations were opened at Plumpton and Cook's Bridge. The line was electrified on 7 July 1935 and remains open with contemporary services provided by the Southern franchise.
- Three Bridges-Horsham – Authorised in 1845, the 8.5-mile long branch from Three Bridges to Horsham opened on 14 February 1848. The line was electrified on 3 July 1938 as part of the Mid-Sussex scheme. Services are currently provided by the Southern franchise.
- Eastbourne – The branch from Polegate to the town of Eastbourne opened on 14 May 1849. The original, relatively primitive, station was replaced by a new structure slightly to the east in 1866. This new station was itself replaced in 1886 by the present structure. The triangular junction at the branch's northern end was completed by the opening of a south-east connection on 1 August 1871. The only intermediate station on the branch, Hampden Park (originally Willingdon), opened on 1 January 1888. The Eastbourne branch was electrified on 7 July 1935. The Polegate 'B'-Stone Cross Junction section, at the northern end of the branch, was to close completely on 6 January 1969, although it was used by engineering trains until the junction was actually severed at Polegate on 8 September 1974.
- Brighton (Kemp Town) – This line was authorised on 13 May 1864 and opened on 2 August 1869. Although only one mile and 32 chains in length, the line contained a 14-arch viaduct and a 1,024yd tunnel. In 1910 there was a frequent service, half-hourly for the bulk of the day with a similar level of service on Sundays. The journey time to and from Brighton Central was about 10min. The line was to suffer eventually from the development of Brighton's tram network and passenger services were withdrawn on 2 January 1933, although Kemp Town remained open for freight traffic until 14 June 1971.
- Cliftonville spur (Brighton) – This short section of track, which allowed access from the main line from London and Brighton to the coastal route towards Shoreham, was opened on 1 July 1879. Electrified on 1 January 1931, the spur remains operational, with passenger services operated by the Southern franchise.
- Hardham Junction to Arundel Junction – The LBSCR obtained powers to construct 17 miles of line from Hardham Junction, on the Horsham-Petworth line to Arundel Junction on 12 July 1858. The line opened on 3 August 1863. The line was electrified as part of the Mid-Sussex scheme on 3 July 1938.

- Littlehampton branch – the 2.5-mile long branch opened on 17 August 1863, although the contemporary layout at Ford Junction, which permits through running to Worthing and Horsham, was opened on 1 January 1887. Services over the branch were electrified on 3 July 1938. The line remains open with services provided by the Southern franchise.
- Newhaven-Seaford – The 2.5-mile long extension from Newhaven to Seaford was opened on 1 June 1864. The line was originally constructed as single track but was doubled in 1905. There was one intermediate station – Bishopstone – which was relocated further to the south on 26 September 1936 (the original station reopened briefly as Bishopstone Beach Halt between 1939 and 1942). The branch was electrified from 7 July 1935 and remains open with services provided by the Southern franchise. The section from Newhaven to Seaford is now singled.
- Shoreham Junction to Itchingfield Junction – The 17-mile long branch via Steyning was authorised on 12 July 1858 and opened from Shoreham Junction to Partridge Green on 1 July 1861 and thence to Itchingfield Junction on 16 September 1861. The line was originally constructed as single track but was doubled between 1877 and 1879. Six intermediate stations were provided. In 1910 there were 10 return workings per weekday with an additional service on Wednesdays only from Henfield to Brighton. There were two return workings on Sunday. A single journey from Brighton to Horsham was timed to take just over an hour for the 26-mile journey. One of the lines threatened by the Beeching Report, passenger services were withdrawn on 7 March 1966 at which time the line from the cement works at Beeding north to Itchingfield Junction closed completely. The final section from Shoreham Junction to Beeding closed on 26 March 1988.

London, Chatham & Dover Railway

Established out of the East Kent Railway on 1 August 1859, the LC&DR was to lead a somewhat parlous financial existence for much of its early life. However, by the early 1870s its financial position had recovered with the result that it merged with the Kent Coast Railway and others. It was to form a joint committee with the South Eastern Railway on 1 August 1899.

Right: Crawley was one of the original intermediate stations when the line opened from Three Bridges to Horsham on 14 February 1848. The original station, pictured here on 27 July 1968, was closed the following day when services were transferred to a new station located slightly to the north. *John Scrace*

Left: Littlehaven, recorded here when it still possessed the 'Halt' suffix on 21 April 1968, was originally opened as Rusper Road Crossing Halt on 1 June 1907. *John Scrace*

Right: A '4COR' EMU arrives at Eastbourne from the Hastings direction. The locomotive-hauled stock visible on the right had arrived at the station earlier on a pensioners' holiday special from Newcastle. *Michael H. C. Baker*

Left: An LBSCR passenger service awaits departure from the terminus of the short Kemp Town branch; increasing competition from Brighton's tram network resulted in the gradual loss of passenger traffic and passenger services ceased in early 1933. *Ian Allan Library*

Right: Following the loss of passenger traffic, the Kemp Town branch was retained for freight services until complete closure in mid-1971. Towards the end of the branch's life, on 3 April 1969, Class 09 shunter No 3669 is recorded in operation at the terminus. *J. M. Tolson*

Left: Although less than two miles in length, the Kemp Town branch included a 1,024yd long tunnel and a 14-arch viaduct. On 28 September 1958 'C2X' 0-6-0 No 32449 heads southward across Lewes Road viaduct with empty coaching stock operated in connection with a civil defence exercise at Kemp Town. *W. M. J. Jackson*

Right: Littlehampton station viewed towards the buffer stops in 1947. *Ian Allan Library*

Left: Viewed looking towards the buffer stops at Seaford on 28 September 1969, '4COR' unit No 3119 can be seen on the left and '2BIL' No 2103 on the right awaiting their next duties.
John Scrace

Right: Southwater was the first intermediate station south of Itchingfield Junction on the route to Shoreham. On 22 April 1964 Ivatt 2-6-2T No 41326 pauses at the station with the 4.21pm service from Horsham to Brighton.
John Scrace

Left: On 30 April 1964 Ivatt 2-6-2T No 41301 is pictured at West Grinstead with the 1.30pm service from Brighton to Horsham.
John Scrace

Right: Partridge Green pictured on 22 April 1964 sees Ivatt 2-6-2T No 41287 hauling the 1.21pm service from Horsham to Brighton. *John Scrace*

Lydd Railway

Nominally independent but absorbed by the SER on 20 September 1895, the Lydd Railway was authorised to construct a line from Appledore to Dungeness in 1881 and from there to New Romney one year later. Passenger and freight services over the line to Lydd commenced on 7 December 1881 with freight to Dungeness commencing at the same date. Passenger services to Dungeness were opened on 1 April 1883. The New Romney branch opened on 19 June 1884. The original New Romney branch was replaced by the SR's realignment on 4 July 1937, on which date passenger services to Dungeness were also withdrawn. The line between Lydd and Dungeness was lifted in January 1952 although a section was later reinstated to serve the nuclear power station. Passenger services over the remainder of the route were withdrawn on 6 March 1967 but the section from Appledore to Dungeness power station remains open to convey nuclear flask traffic.

Maidstone & Ashford Railway

Authorised on 12 August 1880, the M&AR, a subsidiary of the LC&DR, was empowered to construct an 18.75-mile line from Maidstone, where it formed an end-on connection with the Sevenoaks, Maidstone & Tonbridge Railway, to Ashford. The line opened on 1 July 1884. In Ashford, despite the company having obtained running powers into the SER station, the M&AR constructed its own terminus; it was not until 1 November 1891 that the connecting line opened although the LC&DR station did not finally close for a further eight years. The line was electrified as part of the Kent Coast scheme on 18 June 1962 and remains open with contemporary passenger services operated by the South Eastern franchise.

Margate Railway

On 13 August 1859 the Herne Bay & Faversham Railway was empowered to extend its planned line to Margate. The line opened from Faversham to

Left: The first station east of Maidstone on the line towards Ashford is Bearsted; photographed here in 1950 whilst known as Bearsted & Thurnham, the station is at the start of the 1 in 60 descent to Maidstone East.
Ian Allan Library

Whitstable on 1 August 1860 and thence to Herne Bay on 13 July 1861. Following authorisation of the extension from Margate to Ramsgate, the company was renamed the Kent Coast Railway, under whose aegis the section from Herne Bay eastwards was opened. The Faversham-Herne Bay section was electrified as part of the first phase of the Kent Coast scheme on 15 June 1959. Today passenger services are provided by the South Eastern franchise.

Mid-Sussex Railway

The Mid-Sussex Railway was empowered on 10 August 1857 to construct a 17.5-mile single-track branch from Horsham to Coultershaw Mill, near Petworth. Leased to the LBSCR from 1 August 1859, the line opened throughout on 10 October 1859. The LBSCR formally absorbed the line on 29 July 1864. The section from Horsham to Hardham Junction, where the line to Petworth

Left: There was originally one intermediate passenger station on the line between Faversham and Herne Bay – at Whitstable – which opened with the line on 1 August 1860. Known as Whitstable & Tankerton since 1 February 1936, the station is recorded looking towards the west in this view dated 9 September 1968.
John Scrace

diverted from the route to Arundel Junction via Amberley (opened on 3 August 1863), was doubled prior to the completion of the later route. In 1910 there were eight trains a weekday in each direction from Pulborough to Midhurst, with an additional service on Monday mornings from Midhurst to Pulborough and two return workings on Sunday. The journey time was about 24min for the 11-mile single journey. The section of line from Horsham to Hardham Junction was electrified as part of the Mid-Sussex scheme on 3 July 1938. Passenger services over the section of line from Midhurst to Hardham Junction via Petworth were withdrawn on 7 February 1955 and the section between Petworth and Hardham Junction closed completely on 23 May 1966.

Right: Viewed looking westwards from the LBSCR station in Midhurst, this view from the early 1920s illustrates well the inter-relationship between the LBSCR and LSWR lines in the town. On the extreme left a two-coach train headed by a 'D3' class heads towards the LBSCR station from Chichester. In the centre is the connecting line between the LSWR and LBSCR with, on the right, the LSWR engine shed. The LSWR line towards Petersfield can be seen heading towards the west. The LSWR station is out of view to the right of the photographer.
Chris Turner

Right: In April 1947, shortly before Nationalisation, a Midhurst-Horsham train awaits departure from the ex-LBSCR station at Midhurst behind 'D3' class 0-6-0 No 2387.
R. A. H. Baxter

Above: After closure to passenger services, the line remained open for freight traffic. On 23 March 1960, Class C2X 0-6-0 No 32523 passes Selham with the thrice-weekly freight from Midhurst heading towards Pulborough. *Derek Cross*

Left: On 20 August 1978 '4VEP' No 7721 departs from Arundel station with the 13.05 service from Victoria to Bognor Regis. The station opened originally on 3 August 1863. In the foreground can be seen the 1938-built signalbox, which replaced an earlier structure as part of the Mid-Sussex electrification scheme. *Les Bertram*

Mid-Sussex & Midhurst Junction Railway

Incorporated on 13 August 1859, the M&MJR was empowered to construct a line from Petworth westwards to Midhurst and Petersfield. The single-track line was opened as far as Midhurst on 15 October 1866 and by eight years later was taken over the LBSCR. At Midhurst a connection was eventually made with the Chichester & Midhurst Railway. Passenger services over the Midhurst-Petworth section were withdrawn on 7 February 1955 with the line from Midhurst to Petworth closing completely on 12 October 1964.

Oxted & Groombridge Railway

Authorised on 11 August 1881, the O&GR, backed by the LBSCR, was empowered to build 12 miles of line from Hurst Green Junction, on the Oxted-East Grinstead line, to Ashurst Junction on the line between Tunbridge Wells and East Grinstead. It opened between Hurst Green Junction and Edenbridge on 2 January 1888 and thence to Ashurst Junction on 1 October 1888. Intermediate stations were provided at Edenbridge, Hever and Cowden. The line remains open as part of the route to Uckfield with passenger services now provided by the South Eastern franchise.

Below: Hever was one of the intermediate stations opened with the line on 1 October 1888. The station is recorded here, looking towards the north in 1948. *Ian Allan Library*

Petersfield Railway

Although the Mid-Sussex & Midhurst Railway was initially authorised to construct the single-track link from Midhurst to Petersfield, this 9.5-mile long route was actually constructed by the Petersfield Railway, authorised on 23 July 1860, and, following acquisition by the LSWR on 22 June 1863, was opened throughout on 1 September 1864. The original act precluded the PR from operating into the existing station at Midhurst and so the LSWR constructed its own terminus in the town; this was to remain open until 13 July 1925 when services were diverted into the ex-LBSCR station. In 1910 the LSWR operated nine return workings per weekday with three on Sundays. The single journey over the 6.25-mile long route took just over 20min. Passenger services between Petersfield and Midhurst were withdrawn on 7 February 1955, with the line closing completely from the same date.

Left: With the ex-LSWR station in Midhurst in the background Class C2X 0-6-0 No 32526 shunts across the connecting line. Passenger services were transferred from the LSWR station to the ex-LBSCR station in 1925 following the Grouping of 1923.
J. Spencer Gilks

Romney, Hythe & Dymchurch Railway

Constructed to the gauge of 15in by Henry Greenly on behalf of Captain J. E. P. Howey and Count Zbrowski, the RH&DR was officially opened on 16 July 1927 although the complete line was not finished until 1928/29. Boasting to be 'The world's smallest public railway', the RH&DR was under military control between 1940 and 1945, before being returned to private ownership after the cessation of hostilities. The line remains operational.

Rother Valley Light Railway

Authorised on 2 July 1896 as the first railway permitted under the Light Railways Act of 1896, the Rother Valley Light Railway was empowered to

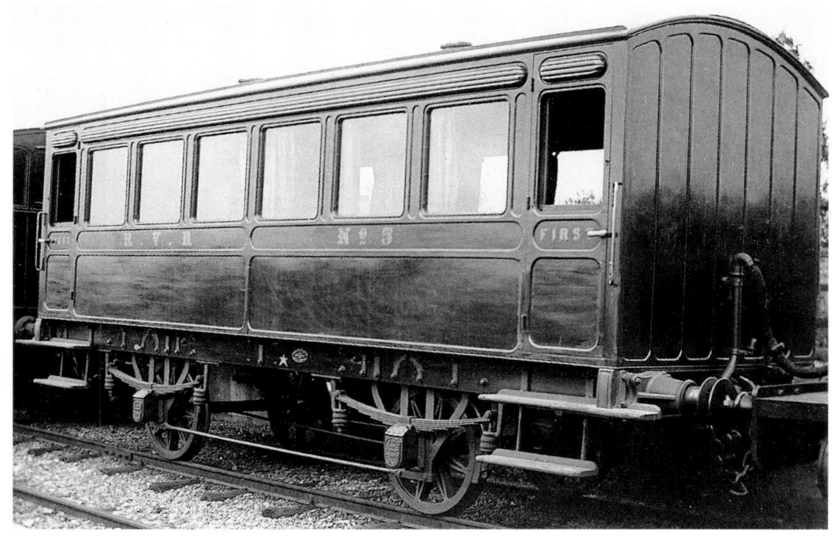

Left: Rother Valley Light Railway first class coach No 5 pictured at Robertsbridge in 1905.
Ian Allan Library

Right: Robertsbridge was the junction for the Kent & East Sussex line to Tenterden. After closure to normal passenger services, seasonal hop-picker specials operated for a number of years and, on 14 September 1957, one such service is pictured – the 12.50pm with 'Terrier' No 32678 at the head – at the junction station prior to departure. Heading towards London on the main line is the new order in the guise of DEMU No 1012 on the Hastings-Charing Cross service. *E. Wilmshurst*

construct a 12-mile long single-track branch from Robertsbridge to Rolvenden and Tenterden. Freight traffic to Rolvenden commenced on 29 March 1900 with passenger services following on 2 April. The extension to Tenterden Town opened on 15 April 1903. In 1903 a further extension, from Tenterden to Headcorn, was authorised, and, in 1904, the company changed its name to the Kent & East Sussex Railway. Passenger services over the line were withdrawn on 4 January 1954, with the original section from Robertsbridge (Hodson's Siding) to Tenterden Town closing completely on 12 June 1961. The spur serving Hodson's Flour Mill was to survive until 1 January 1970. The section from Tenterden southwards has been progressively reopened by the preserved Kent & East Sussex as far as Bodiam and there are plans for a further extension to reconnect with the National Network at Robertsbridge.

Right: In order to cut costs as traffic declined after World War 1, the Kent & East Sussex invested in three petrol-driven railcars, two manufactured by Ford and the third by Shefflex. The first of three, built by Ford in 1923, is recorded at Tenterden Town station. The railcars were not a success, being unpopular with passengers, and all were withdrawn by the outbreak of war in 1939. *Ian Allan Library*

Above: One of the Rye & Camber's two 2-4-0T steam locomotives, *Victoria* (built by Bagnall at Stafford and delivered in 1897), stands at Rye station. *Victoria* was the larger of the two locomotives built for use on the line. The locomotive was sold for scrap in 1932 following the delivery of a petrol-driven locomotive.
Ian Allan Library

Rye & Camber Tramways Company

Incorporated in 1895 with capital of £2,800, the two-mile long Rye & Camber was a 3ft 0in gauge line engineered by Holman Stephens. It opened from Rye to Camber Golf Links – which was linked to Rye Harbour by ferry – on 13 July 1895 and a half-mile extension to Camber Sands opened on 13 July 1908. The line was requisitioned in 1939 but, despite being returned to its original owners, services did not resume after the war.

Sevenoaks Railway

Backed by the LC&DR, the Sevenoaks Railway was authorised to construct six miles of line from Swanley to Sevenoaks – the station now known as Bat & Ball – on 1 August 1859. The line opened throughout on 2 June 1862; on 17 July 1862 powers to extend the route from a junction south of Otford to Maidstone were obtained and the company's name changed to the Sevenoaks, Maidstone & Tunbridge Railway. The line, electrified from Swanley to Sevenoaks on 6 January 1935, remains open with passenger services now provided by the South Eastern franchise.

Sevenoaks, Maidstone & Tunbridge Railway

Authorised on 17 July 1862, the SM&TR was empowered to extend the Sevenoaks Railway's route from south of Otford to Maidstone. Promoted by the LC&DR, the line opened on 1 June 1874 and was absorbed by the LC&DR following an Act of 30 June 1879. The Otford-Maidstone line was electrified from 2 July 1939. The line remains open with passenger services provided by the South Eastern franchise.

Right: When the line opened from Otford to Maidstone, the SM&TR's station in the town was a terminus; it was not for a further ten years that the extension to Ashford was opened, by which time the company had become part of the LC&DR. This picture of Maidstone East, taken in June 1939, shows the view towards Otford shortly before the line was electrified.
Ian Allan Library

Sheppey Light Railway

Authorised on 3 April 1899, the SLR was an 8.75-mile long single-track branch from Queenborough to Leysdown. Built by Colonel Holman Stephens, the SLR was operated from opening on 1 August 1901 (although actually owned after 31 October 1905) by the LC&DR'. In 1910 there were six return workings per weekday with two on Sundays. The single journey took just over 30min. Although there was some residential development along the line, freight traffic was limited and the passenger traffic never grew in line with expectations. The passenger service was withdrawn on 4 December 1950, at which time the line was to be closed completely.

Below: An ex-LC&DR 0-4-4T runs round its train at Leysdown station, terminus of the Sheppey Light Railway. Passenger services over this 8.75-mile long branch were withdrawn on 4 December 1950.
P. Ransome-Wallis

Left: Recorded shortly after Nationalisation, ex-SECR Class R1 0-4-4T No 31696 enters Brambledown station with a service for Leysdown. The locomotive, built in 1900, was withdrawn in 1951.
P. Ransome-Wallis

Sittingbourne & Sheerness Railway

Empowered to construct a seven-mile single-track branch from Sittingbourne to Sheerness and incorporated on 7 July 1856, the S&SR opened on 19 July 1860 and was operated by the LC&DR from the start. The line was extended from Queenborough to Queenborough Pier, to connect with a steamer service to Flushing, on 15 May 1876; this line closed to passenger services in October 1914 although it was briefly revived between 27 December 1922 and 1 March 1923. A second extension saw the line extended to a new station in Sheerness-on-Sea on 1 June 1883. The Sheerness branch was electrified as part of the first phase of the Kent Coast scheme, with electric services being introduced on 15 June 1959. Passenger services are today operated by the South Eastern

Below: On 26 May 1981, a four-car EMU made up of two Class 2HAP units awaits departure from the terminus at Sheerness with the 10.38 service to Sittingbourne.
Brian Morrison

Right: On 25 May 1958, Whit Sunday, Ivatt 2-6-2T No 41309 departs from Sheerness with the 6.33pm special to Sittingbourne whilst, on the left, No 31749 pilots No 31506 on the 6.50pm service to Victoria. Although services are still steam-hauled at this date, evidence of the forthcoming electrification can be seen in the presence of the newly installed conductor rails. *S. C. Nash*

franchise. There remains freight traffic as well, with the docks at Sheerness still rail connected along with paper, steel and other traffic.

South Eastern Railway

Although known as the South Eastern, the railway was incorporated as the London, Deptford & Dover Railway. The line was ultimately constructed from a junction with the LBSCR at Redhill, opening to Headcorn on 31 August 1842, thence to Ashford on 1 December 1842, to Folkestone on 18 December 1843 and finally to Dover on 7 February 1844. In 1899 the SER joined with the LC&DR to form the SECR. The SER's station in Dover became known as Dover Town in 1861 and was to close in 1914. Apart from this section, the entire line remains open, having been electrified from Redhill to Tonbridge in May 1994 and from Tonbridge to Dover on 18 June 1962. The SER constructed a number of additional lines directly. These included:

- Folkestone Harbour branch – Work started on the construction of the branch in 1843 and the short line was opened to freight traffic the same year; passenger services were introduced on 1 January 1849. The line was electrified as part of the second phase of the Kent Coast scheme on 18 June 1962. Although its importance has diminished as a result of the completion of the Channel Tunnel and the withdrawal of ferries from the port, the line remains officially open for special traffic only although little used and increasingly derelict. Ordinary passenger traffic ceased in 2001.
- Paddock Wood to Maidstone – This was the SER's first major branch and was authorised in 1843. The single track line was opened on 25 September 1844 and doubled two years later. In 1853 powers were obtained to extend the line 10.75 miles to Strood, with the line extension opening on 18 June 1856. The line from Paddock Wood to Strood was electrified in two stages: Strood to Maidstone West on 2 July 1939 and Paddock Wood to Maidstone

West on 15 June 1959. Passenger services are currently operated as part of the South Eastern franchise.

- Ashford-Margate – Authorised on 23 May 1844, the line opened from Ashford to Canterbury (West) on 6 February 1846, to Ramsgate (Town) on 13 April 1846 and to Margate (Sands) on 1 December 1846. The line from Margate Sands to Ramsgate closed to passenger services on 2 July 1926 with the opening of the new line in Ramsgate. A new goods depot was constructed to the south of the town and this section of line was to survive until final closure in November 1976. The remainder of the route was electrified as part of the Kent Coast scheme on 18 June 1962.
- Minster-Deal – The branch from Minster to Deal opened on 1 July 1847. Deal was to remain a terminus until 15 June 1881 when the line to Dover was opened. There was one intermediate station, Sandwich, which opened with the line in July 1847. The route was electrified as part of the Kent Coast scheme on 18 June 1962.
- Tonbridge-Hastings – Authorised in 1845, the 5.75-mile long branch from Tonbridge to Tunbridge Wells opened to a temporary station at Jackwoods Spring on 20 September with the short section through the 823yd-long Wells Tunnel to Tunbridge Wells itself following on 25 November 1846. The one intermediate station, called Southborough until 1925, opened in 1893. The 27.25-mile long section southwards from Tunbridge Wells opened as far as Robertsbridge on 1 September 1851, thence to Battle on 1 January 1852 and the final section to Bopeep Junction followed on 1 February 1852. As a result of restricted loading gauge in a number of the tunnels along the route, narrow rolling stock had to be supplied for the route, including the Hastings DEMUs. Following modification, the Tonbridge-Hastings line was electrified with services commencing on 27 April 1986.
- North Kent line – Authorised in 1846, the 22.5-mile long line was designed to provide a link from North Kent East Junction, near London Bridge, via Lewisham and Dartford to Gravesend to connect with the seven miles of line operated by the Thames & Medway Canal to Strood. The canal company was acquired by the SER later in 1846 and the line was opened on 30 July 1849. The SER's Rochester station was in Strood with a ferry connection across the river. The line to Gravesend was electrified in 1930 with the section between there and Rochester being electrified from June 1939. Passenger services are operated today by the South Eastern franchise.
- Ashford-Hastings – The 28-mile long line from Ashford to Hastings opened on 13 February 1851 albeit not without controversy as the LBSCR opened a quarter mile extension to Bopeep Junction on the same day. It was not until 5 December 1870 that SER trains were permitted to stop at St Leonards (Warrior Square). Although threatened with closure under the Beeching Report and subsequently, the Ashford-Hastings line still operates although the section from Appledore south to Hastings is now singled. DMU services are operated as part of the South Eastern franchise. At Rye a short branch was constructed to serve the harbour; this opened in 1854 and was to survive until closure on 29 February 1960.

- St Johns-Tonbridge – This 24-mile route, designed to shorten the distance by SER between London and Dover, was authorised on 30 June 1862. The line opened from St Johns to Chislehurst on 1 July 1865, the entire route being opened for freight traffic on 3 February 1868 with the line opening for passenger services from Chislehurst to Sevenoaks on 2 March 1868 and thence to Tonbridge on 1 May 1868. The line reduced the distance between London and Tonbridge by 12.5 miles. The route was electrified as far as Sevenoaks on 6 January 1935 and thence to Tonbridge on 18 June 1962.
- Chatham Central branch – This opened, with a new bridge across the Medway, from Strood to Rochester on 20 July 1891 and to Chatham Central on 1 March 1892. As such it paralleled the LC&DR route to Rochester and, following the creation of the SECR, rationalisation followed. Passenger services to Rochester Common and Chatham Central were withdrawn on 1 October 1911 although the bulk of the line remained open to serve the goods depot at Chatham. At the western end, all services were diverted to use the newer bridge following the realignment of the ex-LC&DR route in 1927 and the original bridge was converted for use by road traffic.
- Sandgate branch – The 3.5-mile long branch from Sandling Junction through Hythe to Sandgate opened on 9 October 1874. Powers were obtained two years later for the construction of an extension to Folkestone Harbour, but this was never constructed. In 1910 there were 15 services per weekday from Sandling Junction to Sandgate (17 on Saturdays; 11 on Sundays) with 13 from Sandgate on Tuesdays to Fridays (14 on Mondays; 15 on Saturdays; 11 on Sundays) with a single journey taking about eight minutes. Passenger services from Hythe to Sandgate were withdrawn on 1 April 1931 and between Sandling Junction and Hythe were suspended between 23 May 1943 and 1 October 1945, being withdrawn on 3 December 1951 on which date the line closed completely.

Right: Just to the west of the ex-SER station in Edenbridge, the line crosses over the LBSCR route from Hurst Green Junction to Eridge. Here 'C' class No 31724 pilots an unidentified 'N' class Mogul on the 3.20pm goods from Tonbridge to Redhill over the bridge above the ex-LBSCR route. *Derek Cross*

Left: Penshurst was one of the original stations when the line opened from Redhill to Headcorn in 1842 although the station, as illustrated here looking towards the west on 11 September 1968, was subsequently rebuilt. *John Scrace*

Right: The down 'Golden Arrow' powers its way through Paddock Wood behind 'Battle of Britain' class Pacific No 34086 *219 Squadron*. *Derek Cross*

Left: On 7 April 1980, Easter Monday, Class 47 No 47539 passes Ashford with the 08.00 service from Alfreton to Folkestone. This scene is now radically altered as a result of the construction of the International platforms serving Eurostar services to and from Paris or Brussels. *Peter Kynaston*

Right: Folkestone Central recorded in July 1960 sees work in hand for the reconstruction of the station in connection with the second phase of the Kent Coast electrification scheme.
Ian Allan Library

Below: Between Folkestone and Dover, the SER constructed its line along the foreshore with tunnels at Martello, Abbotscliffe and Shakespeare. This view, taken in 1931, shows the eastern portals to Shakespeare Tunnel. The foreshore at this location has been altered through the depositing of spoil from the construction of the Channel Tunnel, the route of which passes directly beneath the earlier tunnel.
Ian Allan Library

Left: Yalding was one of the intermediate stations opened with the SER's branch from Tonbridge to Maidstone on 25 September 1844. Here, on 30 June 1976, Class 73 No 73006 heads towards Tonbridge with the 15.02 freight from Hoo Junction.
R. I. Wallace

Right: The first intermediate station north of Maidstone on the line towards Strood is Aylesford, which opened with the line in June 1856. The original station building, just restored at the date of the photograph, was constructed from Kentish ragstone with Caen stone dressing.
On 21 October 1988, the last unit to be repainted in the attractive but short-lived 'Jaffa cake' livery, '4CEP' No 1619 is recorded arriving at the station with the 13.53 from Paddock Wood to Strood. Visible behind the unit is the 1921-built signalbox that controls the level crossing.
Brian Morrison

Left: Snodland is one of the intermediate stations located on the SER's extension from Maidstone West to Strood.
On 13 September 1986, two Class 416/4s, Nos 6401 and 6406, arrive at the station with the 13.53 service from Paddock Wood to Strood.
Chris Wilson

Right: Wye is the first intermediate station on the line from Ashford to Margate. On 8 April 1953 'L' class 4-4-0 No 31781 arrives at the station at the head of the 10.10am service from Margate to Ashford. *Donald Kelk*

Left: On 8 April 1953 Class 4 2-6-4T No 42067 arrives at Chilham with the 9.42am stopping service from Ashford to Margate. *Donald Kelk*

Right: Canterbury West station recorded in 1947. *Ian Allan Library*

Left: The first station on the section of line from Canterbury to Minster is Sturry, recorded here looking towards the east from the up platform on 2 April 1953. *Donald Kelk*

Right: Minster is the location of the triangular junction between the Canterbury-Ramsgate line and that from Minster southwards to Deal and Dover. This view, taken looking towards the west, shows the station on 4 September 1968. *John Scrace*

Left: The terminus of the line from Canterbury to Ramsgate was Ramsgate Town station, viewed here from the buffer stops in 1924. This was shortly before the station closed with the opening of the link line via Dumpton Park. *Ian Allan Library*

Right: After closure, the original SER station in Margate – Sands – was converted into a restaurant as shown in this 1932 view. *Ian Allan Library*

Left: The original station at Deal opened on 1 July 1847 and was designed as a terminus station. It became a through station with the completion of the line to Dover in 1881. *Ian Allan Library*

Right: Viewed looking towards the north in May 1959, this view of Deal shows a train arriving from the Mindster junction direction past the 1939-built signalbox. Dominating the centre of the photograph is the engine shed that originally served the station. First opened in 1847, the shed was extended and reopened in 1881 and provided with a 50ft turntable. The shed was to close in September 1930, being used as a goods shed thereafter before final closure shortly after this photograph was taken. The building was subsequently demolished and the site redeveloped. *Ian Allan Library*

Left: On 16 August 1960, Type 3 No D6510 takes the through road at Tonbridge with a freight service to London. *John Scrace*

Right: Originally known as Ticehurst Road, the station was renamed Stonegate on 16 June 1947. With evidence of the new electrified order all too evident, DEMU No 1012 forms the 13.45 service from Charing Cross to Hastings on 15 March 1986. A month later services over the route were replaced by EMUs. *John Scrace*

Left: With work on electrification yet to commence at this point, one of the Class 33/2s specifically designed for use over the route, No 33201, is recorded on 13 April 1984 with a train of empty gypsum wagons destined for Mountfield. *R. S. Freeman*

Above: The last station on the Tonbridge-Hastings line is West St Leonards. The station, which opened in 1887, is recorded towards Bopeep Junction looking south in this 1931 view.
Ian Allan Library

Above: Northfleet station opened in 1849. This view shows the station as it existed on 12 September 1969.
John Scrace

Left: When the SER first reached Strood the station, called Rochester, was on the west bank of the Medway and Rochester itself, with its cathedral and castle visible in the distance, was served by ferry. Apart from the passenger station, the town's docks were also rail served as shown in this view taken on 3 March 1968 as a Class 73 hauls the LCGB 'Invicta' rail tour past the SR-built signalbox. Also visible, behind the signalbox, is the 1856-built engine shed; this had been closed in 1939 and converted into a goods shed. The building was destined to be demolished later in 1970.
Stephen May

Left: The station at Strood was relocated in 1856 when the line to Maidstone was opened. This 1914 view, looking towards the south, sees the connection towards Rochester across the Medway heading off towards the left whilst the line towards Maidstone heads southwards past the signalbox and under the ex-LC&DR line from Swanley Junction to Rochester.
Ian Allan Library

Left: Two Class 202 DEMUs, Nos 1011 and 1031, are recorded running ecs through St Leonards (Warrior Square) on 28 August 1977.
Les Bertram

Right: Opened originally on 13 February 1851, Hastings was used by both the SER and by the LBSCR. This 1931 view is taken looking towards the west. *Ian Allan Library*

Left: Located on the outskirts of Hastings and the first intermediate station on the line to Ashford, Ore is also the easternmost terminus of the third-rail electrification along the route in order to provide access to the depot shown in the background to this view taken on 17 August 1981. Two Class 2HAP units, with No 6016 in the foreground, have just arrived with a stopping service from Brighton. *John Glover*

Right: The disused platform at Winchelsea viewed towards Hastings on 22 April 1989. *Nigel Hunt*

Left: DEMU No 1034 passes the 1894-built SER signalbox at Rye with a service from Hastings to Ashford. The Italianate station building dates from 1851. Today, Rye is the passing loop on the single-track section between Ore and Appledore. *Ian Allan Library*

Right: The cut-off route via Sevenoaks was to reduce the distance between London and Tonbridge by more than 12 miles, but the new route was heavily engineered with several tunnels, including the 3,454yd-long tunnel at Sevenoaks. Immediately to the north of the tunnel is Sevenoaks station. The station is recorded here after the electrification of the line northwards in 1935 when the name was Sevenoaks (Tubs Hill); the station was renamed Sevenoaks only in 1950. *Ian Allan Library*

Left: Sandling Junction was the point at which the short Sandgate branch headed to the south off the SER main line. As a double-headed service from Margate to Charing Cross passes through the station headed by Type 3 No D6527 piloting Type 2 No D5002, the stub of the branch can be seen curving away. In the distance can be seen two Pullman coaches; these were used as holiday coaches at the station. *M. Edwards*

South Eastern & Chatham Railway Companies Joint Management Committee

Formed on 1 August 1899, this was a joint committee of the SER and LC&DR although both of the constituent companies maintained their individual ownership. The SECR became part of the Southern Railway at Grouping in 1923.

Right: There were only a handful of developments affecting the railway network of the area after the creation of the SECR and before the creation of the Southern Railway in 1923. One of these was the completion of the replacement Dover Admiralty Pier station on 2 February 1915. The station was renamed Dover Marine on 5 December 1918 prior to opening on 18 January 1919. It was renamed Dover Western Docks on 14 May 1979 and was finally closed on 26 September 1994. This Southern Railway era view sees 'King Arthur' class 4-6-0 No 766 awaiting departure. *Ian Allan Library*

Southern Railway

Established as one of the 'Big Four' companies at the Grouping in 1923, the Southern Railway promoted the construction of a number of lines. These included, in Kent and Sussex, the following routes:

- Ramsgate – The 1.5-mile long line from Broadstairs to a connection on the Minster-Ramsgate line allowed for the closure of the Ramsgate-Margate Sands route and of Ramsgate Town and Harbour stations. The new line, with intermediate stations at Dumpton Park and Ramsgate, was opened on 2 July 1926. The line was electrified from the north to Ramsgate on 15 June 1959 and from the Canterbury direction on 18 June 1962.
- Allhallows-on-Sea branch – Opened on 14 May 1932, the branch, some 1.75 miles in length, ran from Stoke Junction, on the Hoo Junction-Port Victoria line, to Allhallows-on-Sea. The line, constructed as double track, was part of the SR's efforts to try and encourage the growth of the town as a resort and most of the passenger services that had previously served Port Victoria were diverted to the new terminus. However, this was not to prove a success and passenger services over the branch were withdrawn on 4 December 1961, at which stage the section from Stoke Junction to Allhallows closed completely.
- New Romney branch – The Southern Railway inherited a branch to New Romney from the SECR. However, the growth in the area's popularity as a destination for holidaymakers resulted in the SR deciding to relocate the

Left: Looking towards the west, this view of the 1926 station at Ramsgate records the scene prior to electrification. On the right can be seen the coaling stage that served the engine shed whilst closer to the station can be seen the carriage shed; this survives in use as an EMU depot. *P. Ransome-Wallis*

Right: Pictured in September 1952, ex-LC&DR 'R' class 0-4-4T No 31662 is recorded taking water at the branch terminus at Allhallows-on-Sea. The locomotive, dating originally from 1891, would be withdrawn the following year whilst passenger services over the branch would last until the early 1960s. *P. Ransome-Wallis*

Left: On 26 May 1960, 'H' class 0-4-4T No 31553 is pictured at Sharnal Street station with a service from Allhallows-on-Sea. Sharnal Street was the junction for the Chattenden Naval Tramway and Kingsnorth Light Railway; by this date the former was approaching the end of its career and the latter had been closed and lifted. The connection to these lines was slightly to the east of the road bridge in this view. *J. A. V. Smallwood*

line closer to the sea. The new alignment, with intermediate stations at Lydd-on-Sea and Greatstone-on-Sea, opened on 4 July 1937. Passenger services to New Romney ceased on 6 March 1967, at which date the line beyond the CEGB terminal at Lydd serving the nuclear power station to New Romney closed completely.

Right: DEMU No 1119 pictured ay New Romney station in December 1965 with a service to Ashford. At this time, the branch had been given a reprieve from closure; this was not, however, to last for long as passenger services were ultimately to be withdrawn on 6 March 1967. *J. A. M. Vaughan*

Right: The 1.52pm service from New Romney to Ashford leaves Lydd Town station on 10 November 1966. The train is formed of three-car DEMU No 1118. *J. A. M. Vaughan*

Tunbridge Wells & Eastbourne Railway

Whilst the first proposals for a link between Polegate and Hailsham dated to the 1840s, it was not until the 1870s that the LBSCR-backed TW&ER progressed. The line was opened from Polegate to Hailsham on 14 May 1879, thence to Heathfield on 5 April 1880 and finally to Eridge on 1 September 1880. Passenger services between Eridge and Hailsham were withdrawn on 14 June

1965, at which time the section from Redgate Mill Junction to Heathfield closed completely. The section from Hailsham to Heathfield closed completely on 26 April 1968 with passenger services between Hailsham and Polegate being withdrawn on 9 September 1968; freight facilities at Hailsham had been withdrawn the previous month, the line closing completely from that date.

Westerham Valley Railway

Backed by the SER (who took it over following an Act of 11 August 1881), the five-mile long single-track branch from Dunton Green to Westerham was authorised on 24 July 1876 and opened on 7 July 1881. When the line was opened, there was one intermediate station – Brasted – but a second, Chevening, was to follow in 1906. In 1910, there were 15 return workings per weekday with the exception of Wednesdays (when there were 17 return workings) and Saturdays (when there were 18 down and 16 up services). There were eight return workings on Sundays. The single journey took just over 10min. The line was to lose its passenger services on 30 October 1961, at which time it closed completely as freight facilities were withdrawn from the same date.

Below: 'R1' class 0-4-4T No 31704 awaits departure from the branch terminus at Westerham with the 12.19pm service to Dunton Green on 22 August 1953.
B. Fletcher

LOCOMOTIVE SHEDS AND FACILITIES

Ashford

The first shed in the town was opened by the SER on 1 December 1842; it survived until 1931 when it was replaced by a new shed south of the station in the 'V' formed by the junction of the lines to Folkestone and Canterbury. The Maidstone & Ashford Railway opened a two-track shed adjacent to its terminus in the town in 1894. The shed closed on 1 January 1899 when the terminus closed. Thereafter it was used as a goods shed until 1971. It was subsequently demolished. The original SER shed was replaced by a new 10-road shed by the SR in 1931; this survived until closure to steam in June 1962. It was used until 1968 as a diesel depot before final closure when an effort to establish a preservation base saw its temporary reuse. Following the failure of the Ashford Steam centre, the building was subsequently demolished over a period of time.

Bexhill

A two-road shed was constructed to the west of Bexhill West station and opened on 1 June 1902. Closed by the SR in 1936, the shed was subsequently used as a council depot.

Bognor Regis

The first shed at Bognor Regis, located on the east side of the line to the north of the station, opened on 1 June 1864; the wooden two-road structure was replaced by a brick building that survived until closure in 1953. Demolished in 1956, the shed site was used for servicing locomotives until 1965.

Brighton

Two small sheds were opened by the London & Brighton Railway early on: the first, dating from 12 May 1840, was to close in 1861 whilst the second, opened on 21 September 1841, was a four–road structure located to the north of the station. This was also closed in 1861 and the site utilised as part of the works. The two original sheds were replaced by a new 16-road shed on the west side of the main line to the north of the station in 1861. This was rebuilt as a 10-road shed in 1938 and was to close on 15 July 1961. The shed was demolished five years later.

Canterbury

The first shed serving the city was that of the Canterbury & Whitstable, which opened in 1830 and closed in 1846. The SER constructed a shed at Canterbury West, which opened on 6 April 1846. This was subsequently rebuilt and was to survive until closure in 1955 and was later demolished. The LC&DR had two small facilities at Canterbury East, both of which opened in 1860; the larger of the two closed largely the following year with the opening of the shed at Dover Priory, although limited facilities were retained thereafter.

Chatham

A servicing point at Chatham was opened by the East Kent Railway on 25 January 1858; it survived until *c*1960.

Chichester

A two-road shed, located to the south of the station, was opened on 8 June 1846; it was to close in the early 1870s.

Deal

The shed was opened by the SER on 1 July 1847 and was subsequently extended. Closed in September 1930, the building was to survive in other railway use until the 1960s when it was demolished and the site redeveloped.

Dover

The first sheds in the town were two constructed by the SER on the approaches to Dover Town station and opened on 14 February 1844. One closed by 1862 when a new facility was opened. The closure dates of the two Dover Town sheds is uncertain, but probably coincided with the closure of Dover Town station on 14 October 1914. The LC&DR shed at Dover Priory opened on 22 July 1861; this was to survive until closure in 1932 and was subsequently demolished. The final shed at Dover – Dover Marine – was opened by the SR in 1928 and was to survive until 12 June 1961. The shed was demolished after closure.

Eastbourne

The first of three sheds in the town opened on 14 May 1849. A two-road shed, sited towards the branch terminus, this facility was replaced by an eight-road semi-roundhouse sited on the north side of the branch in 1876. Although closed in 1912, following the opening of a new seven-road shed further north in 1911, the turntable at the roundhouse remained in use until 1935. The new shed remained open until 1952 and as a servicing point thereafter. Finally completely closed in 1968, the shed was demolished in 1969.

East Grinstead

Opened by the East Grinstead Railway on 9 July 1855, a one-road shed was located on the south side of High Level station. The shed closed in 1896 and the building was demolished a decade later, although servicing continued on the site thereafter.

Faversham

The first shed in the town was opened by the East Kent Railway on 25 January 1858 and was located to the west of the station. This closed in 1895. A second shed, to the east of the station, was opened by the LC&DR in 1860 and was to be extended in 1900. Both sections were reroofed – in 1935 and 1951 respectively – before closure in June 1959, although the newer shed was used for the stabling of diesel locomotives for a period thereafter. Subject to a preservation order, the shed still stands.

Folkestone

Two small single-track sheds were constructed on the south of the line at the east end of Folkestone Junction station and opened on 18 December 1843; this facility was replaced in 1900 by a new three-road shed on the north side of the line. This was to survive until closure on 12 June 1961 and, after a period in use for the stabling of diesels locomotives, was demolished. A single-road shed was established at Folkestone Harbour in 1881; it was relocated in 1899 and again in 1910. The shed closed finally in 1919 but continued in railway use until demolition in *c*1960.

Gillingham

A three-road shed was opened by the LC&DR in 1885 and extended *c*1900. The shed was reroofed in 1931 and was closed by BR on 13 June 1960. The building has been demolished.

Gravesend

A two-road shed was opened on 10 May 1886; the shed closed in 1923.

Hailsham

A one-road shed to the east of the station existed between 1858 and 1880.

Hastings

A three-road shed located to the north of the station opened on 13 February 1851. It was closed in 1929 and replaced by a servicing point as part of the SR's rebuilding of Hastings station.

Hawkhurst

A two-road shed was opened at the branch terminus with the opening of the line on 4 September 1893. The shed officially closed in 1931, although remained available for servicing until the line's closure in 1961.

Haywards Heath

A two-road shed to the east of the station was opened on 1 October 1847; it was converted into a goods shed in the early 1870s.

Horsham

A three-road shed on the west side of the line to the north of the station was opened on 14 February 1848. It was replaced in 1896 by a 10-road semi-roundhouse located on the east side of the line. In 1901 the roundhouse was extended to become an 18-road structure. It was to close to steam on 18 July 1959 and was then used for diesel stabling until final closure in June 1964. The building has been demolished.

Hythe

A two-road shed was constructed for use by the RH&DR at Hythe and opened on 27 July 1927. The shed remains in use as a workshop.

Lancing
A one-road shed was sited within the works at Lancing; it opened in June 1929 and was to survive until the works closed on 28 June 1965.

Lewes
A small shed existed at Lewes between 1853 and 1870; it was then used as a goods shed before to being demolished in 1899 prior to the rebuilding of the station.

Littlehampton
A two-road shed was opened adjacent to the station on 17 August 1863. Closed in 1937, the building was subsequently used as a store and remains in railway use.

Lyminster
Sited to the south of the line to the east of the station, this two-road shed was opened on 16 March 1846 and was to close on 17 August 1863 with the opening of the shed at Littlehampton. The building survived until post-Nationalisation but has been subsequently demolished.

Maidstone
The first shed in the town was opened by the SER slightly to the south of Maidstone West station on 25 September 1844; this was closed on 18 June 1856 and replaced by a second shed further to the south. This was to close in 1933 and be replaced by a stabling point that survived until the line was electrified six years later. The SM&TR opened a shed to the south of Maidstone East station on 1 June 1874; this was to survive until closure by the SR in 1933 after which it was demolished.

Margate
A three-road shed, located to the north of Margate West station, existed between 1865 and 1930 when it was demolished for a parcels depot.

Midhurst
Both the LSWR and LBSCR had facilities in the town. The former's shed, a one-road structure located to the west of the LSWR station, was opened on 1 September 1864. It was to close in 1937. The one-road wooden-built LBSCR shed, located to the north of the LBSCR station, opened on 15 October 1866; it was rebuilt, again in wood, in 1907, and was closed in 1923.

New Romney
Built for the RH&DR, the three-track shed at New Romney opened on 27 July 1927. It remains in use.

Newhaven
A two-road shed was built on the east side of the station and opened on 8 December 1847. It closed in 1887 and was replaced by a new four-road shed to

the west of the station. The building was reroofed prior to 1950 and was to close on 9 September 1963. Now in private hands, the building still stands.

Petworth
Opened on 10 October 1859, the shed was closed on 15 October 1866 and the structure removed for reuse on Hayling Island.

Polegate
Opened c1860, a one-road shed was located to the east of the original Polegate station; this was relocated to the east in 1881 and the shed reduced in size as part of the remodelling of the junction. The facilities remained in use until after Nationalisation.

Ramsgate
The first of three facilities in the town opened on 13 April 1846 on the south side of the line west of Ramsgate Town station; this closed on 2 July 1926. The second facility was a servicing area opened adjacent to the Harbour station on 5 October 1863; this too closed on 2 July 1926. The third facility, opened in 1930, was sited on the north side of the line to the west of the new Ramsgate station. The shed was closed to steam in June 1959 and converted for use by EMUs; it remains in use today.

Rolvenden
The Rother Valley Light Railway constructed a wooden two-road shed, which opened on 29 March 1900. It was later rebuilt in brick and timber before being closed by BR on 4 January 1954. It was later demolished.

Rye
Built by the 3ft 0in gauge Rye & Camber, this one-road shed opened on 13 July 1895. The line was requisitioned in 1939 and, although returned to its original owners after the war, never reopened.

St Leonards
Although a servicing point was established here in 1846 the first documented structure was a two-road building constructed *c*1872. This was rebuilt as a four-road shed in 1898 and reroofed in 1949. Closed in 1958 and used as a diesel stabling point until complete closure in the mid-1960s, steam locomotives were serviced until the withdrawal of steam in the area.

Sandgate
The SER opened a single-track shed on 9 October 1874. The shed closed on 31 December 1921.

Selsey
A two-road timber-built shed was opened by the Selsey Tramway on 27 August 1897. The shed closed with the line on 19 January 1935.

Sevenoaks (Bat & Ball)

Opened by the Sevenoaks Railway on 2 June 1862, this single-track shed passed to the LC&DR on 30 June 1879. Closed by the SR in 1935, the shed was demolished the following year.

Sheerness

A one-road shed was opened with the line on 19 July 1860. The shed was later extended prior to closure in 1915. It was temporarily reopened in 1922, following the failure of the King's Ferry Bridge before final closure the following year.

Shepherd's Well

A two-road timber shed was constructed for the East Kent Light Railway and opened in 1912. The shed closed on 30 October 1948.

Three Bridges

The first shed at the junction was located to the south of the station on the west side. This was opened in July 1848 and was to close in 1909 when the station was enlarged. A replacement shed, located further south, was opened in 1909 and rebuilt as a three-road structure two years later. Closed in July 1964, the site was then used for diesel stabling until final closure in the early 1970s. The building has been demolished.

Tonbridge

The initial three-road shed, located to the east of the station, was first opened on 26 May 1842. The shed was enlarged with a further three-road section prior to 1880. Following further improvements by the SR, the shed was reroofed in 1952. The shed was closed to steam on 17 June 1962 but remained thereafter as a diesel stabling point even after the building's demolition.

Tunbridge Wells West

A two-road shed, to the south of the station, was opened on 1 October 1866; this was to close in 1890 and be replaced by a new four-road shed on the north side of the station. This was rebuilt in 1955 but closed on 9 September 1963. After this it was used to house the BR Emergency Control Train. Following the line's closure, the shed has been used by the Tunbridge Wells & Eridge Railway Preservation Society.

Uckfield

A one road shed existed at Uckfield between 18 October 1858 and 3 August 1868.

Westerham

A timber one-road shed was opened by the Westerham Valley Railway on 7 July 1881. The shed survived until closure in 1926, although servicing facilities remained until the line's closure on 30 October 1961.

LOCOMOTIVE AND OTHER WORKS

Kent and Sussex was home for a number of major workshops, producing locomotives, carriages and wagons.

Ashford

In February 1846, the board of the SER approved the purchase of 185 acres. Construction work commenced the following year and, in 1848, the first locomotive built at the site was completed. By 1899, and the merger with the LC&DR, more than 400 locomotives had been constructed. In 1900, Longhedge Works in London was closed and the work transferred to Ashford with the works being rebuilt between then and 1911. In 1937, the works constructed its first diesel locomotive, following this with its first electric locomotive in 1941. The works built its last steam locomotive in 1944 and its last locomotive in 1952. In July 1962 all locomotive work was transferred to Eastleigh and the works turned to the maintenance of cranes and track maintenance vehicles.

Ashford Wagon Works

Opened by the SER in 1850, the works was designed primarily for the construction and maintenance of wagons; it was amalgamated with the locomotive works in 1962 but was to close in 1982.

Brighton

Opened by the London & Brighton in 1840, becoming the LBSCR's main workshops in 1952, the year in which the site's first locomotive was constructed. It continued to build locomotives through until March 1957, by which date 1,211 locomotives had been built in Brighton. Locomotive work ceased in 1958 and the site was closed completely in 1964 with any remaining work being transferred to Ashford. The site was cleared in 1969 and is now used as a car park.

Lancing

The LBSCR's carriage works was opened in 1888, with work being gradually transferred from Brighton. The works was used primarily for the construction of carriages and wagons. Plans for the maintenance of EMUs at Lancing in the early 1950s were not progressed and the site was to be closed completely on 28 June 1965. The site is now an industrial estate.

THE BEECHING REPORT

Published in 1963, the Beeching Report *The Reshaping of British Railways* recommended that the following lines within Kent and Sussex should have all passenger services removed:

- Ashford (Kent)-Hastings
- Ashford (Kent)-New Romney
- Crowhurst-Bexhill West
- Haywards Heath-Seaford (local)
- Three Bridges-Tunbridge Wells West
- Tonbridge-Brighton
- Tonbridge-Eastbourne
- Brighton-Horsham
- Guildford-Horsham

The following services were to be modified:

- Tunbridge Wells Central-Hastings
- Sheerness-on-Sea-Dover Priory (local)
- Brighton-Ore (local)

Below: The Kent & East Sussex line lost its passenger services in 1954 so did not figure in the Beeching report as to be closed to passenger services. Rolvenden shed is viewed in 1931. *Ian Allan Library*

PRESERVATION

The counties of Kent and Sussex have five preservation sites based upon closed BR lines: the Bluebell Railway, the Kent & East Sussex, the Lavender Line, the East Kent Railway and the Spa Valley Railway. In addition to these, a section of the Bowaters' narrow gauge operation at Sittingbourne is preserved as the Sittingbourne & Kemsley.

The oldest of these operations is the Bluebell. The preserved railway sprang from the closure controversy in the mid-1950s and a desire to see services restored for the full length of the line from Culver Junction to East Grinstead once BR was finally empowered to proceed with closure. The Lewes & East Grinstead Railway Preservation Society was established in early 1959 but the group's initial aims proved too ambitious and the society initially leased the section from Horsted Keynes to Sheffield Park. The first items of rolling stock arrived, under their own steam, on 17 May 1960 with limited services starting that summer, making it the first ex-BR standard gauge line to enter preservation. Ironically, a locomotive from the railway was hired to assist in the dismantling of the line north of Horsted Keynes in 1964. In the mid-1970s thoughts turned towards reconnecting to the BR network at East Grinstead, with the first step being the acquisition of the site of West Hoathly station. In 1985 permission was granted for the extension to East Grinstead. The first phase of the extension, one mile northwards, opened in 1990 and this was followed by the two miles to West Hoathly, reopened in 1992. The extension to Kingscote opened on 23 April 1994 and work is currently in hand to complete the project, although a major barrier remains the fact that Imberhome cutting, south of East Grinstead, was used as a landfill site and some 300,000cu m of waste will need to be removed.

Following closure of the Kent & East Sussex in 1961, a campaign for its preservation was launched. However, there was much opposition from the Ministry of Transport in the late 1960s as the railway crossed a number of major roads between London and the south coast on the level and the project was given the go-ahead only by agreeing to abandon the section from Robertsbridge to Bodiam with its three crossings. As a result it was not until 3 February 1974 that the first three-mile section from Tenterden Town was reopened. The line was extended to Wittersham Road in 1977, to Northiam in 1990 and to Bodiam in 2000. A separate company, the Rother Valley Railway, is campaigning for the restoration of the link from Bodiam to Robertsbridge and is currently working from a base at Robertsbridge laying track from the station.

The smallest of the five sites running over ex-BR lines is the Lavender Line, based at Isfield on the closed Uckfield-Lewes line. The site at Isfield was purchased on 16 June 1983 at auction by Dave and Gwen Milham with the intention of restoring the site and operating a short section of line. The restoration and 0.75-mile long running track was completed in 1987 and the line was acquired from the Milham family by the Lavender Line Preservation Society in 1991 and a short northern extension was opened two years later.

Following closure of the Eridge to Tunbridge Wells line on 6 July 1985, the Tunbridge Wells & Eridge Railway Preservation Society was formed and, following a long campaign, the route was secured in the early 1990s. The line became known as the Spa Valley Railway following merger with the North Downs Steam Railway. The first limited services were operated late in 1996 and have been gradually extended subsequently with services now operating between Tunbridge Wells West and Groombridge. The railway's long-term plans remain to extend to Eridge.

Established in 1985 following the closure of the last section of the erstwhile East Kent Railway, the East Kent Light Railway obtained a Light Railway Order on 31 August 1993 for the reopening of the line from Shepherd's Well to Tilmanstone. Services currently operate between Shepherd's Well and Eythorne.

MAPS

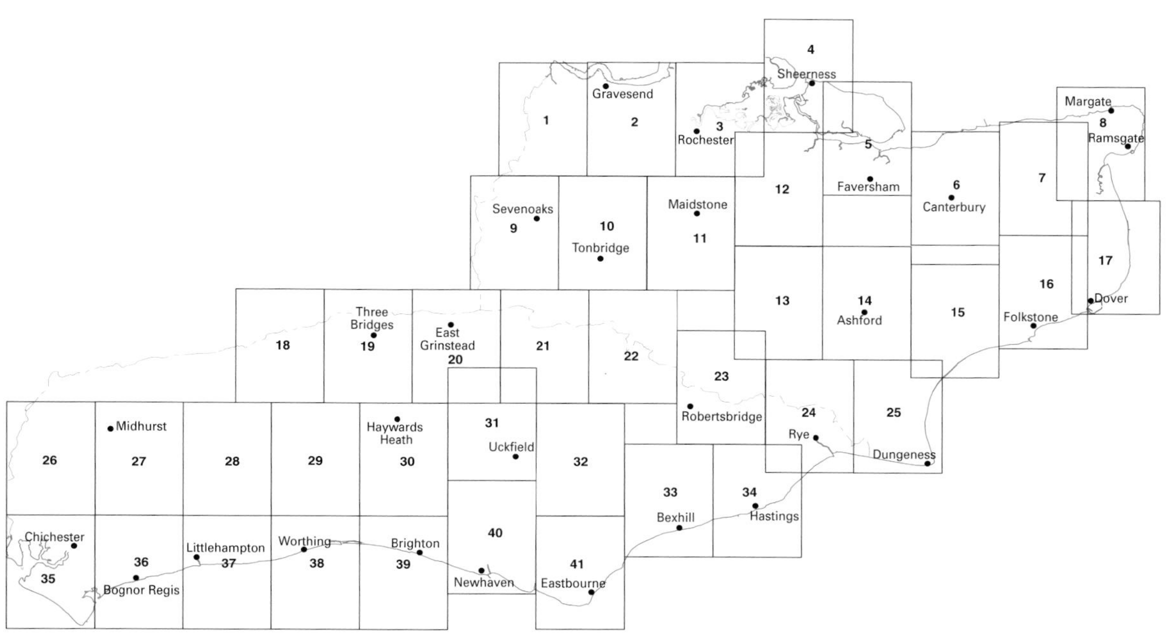

LEGEND			
(line symbol)	Closed line	(black rectangle)	Locomotive shed
(line symbol)	Passenger line	**SOUTH EASTERN**	Railway company name
(line symbol)	Preserved line		**Abbreviations used on maps**
(line symbol)	Freight line	c.	circa (around)
Billingshurst ●	Station open	Clly	Colliery
(1923)	Date station opened	G	Goods
Canterbury South ○	Station closed	HL	High Level (station)
[1964]	Date station closed	LL	Low Level (station)
1857	Date railway line opened	*J*	Junction - used with signalbox name
Clo 1989	Date railway line closed	Junc	Junction - as used in station name
A2	Main road / road number	*Sdg*	Siding
M20	Motorway /motorway junction / motorway number	Std G.	Standard gauge
(symbols)	Level crossing / bridge	Tnl	Tunnel
(symbol)	Water Trough	UL	Uncertain location

MAP ONE

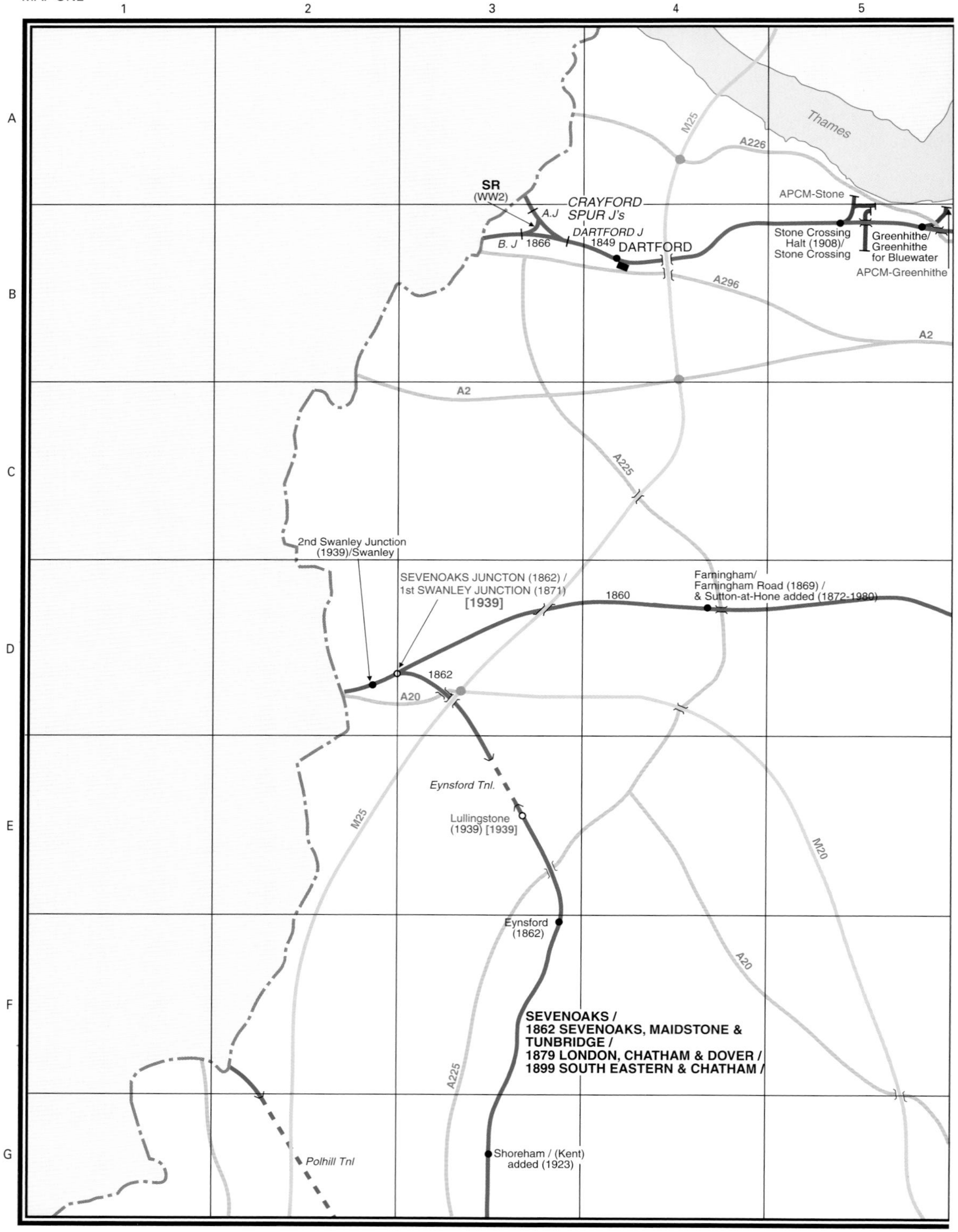

1 2 3 4 5

A B C D E F G

Thames
M25
A226
SR
(WW2)
CRAYFORD
SPUR J's
A.J
B. J
1866
DARTFORD J
1849
DARTFORD
APCM-Stone
Stone Crossing
Halt (1908)/
Stone Crossing
Greenhithe/
Greenhithe
for Bluewater
APCM-Greenhithe
A296
A2
A2
A225
2nd Swanley Junction
(1939)/Swanley
SEVENOAKS JUNCTON (1862) /
1st SWANLEY JUNCTION (1871)
[1939]
1860
Farningham/
Farningham Road (1869) /
& Sutton-at-Hone added (1872-1980)
1862
A20
Eynsford Tnl.
Lullingstone
(1939) [1939]
M25
M20
Eynsford
(1862)
A20
SEVENOAKS /
1862 SEVENOAKS, MAIDSTONE &
TUNBRIDGE /
1879 LONDON, CHATHAM & DOVER /
1899 SOUTH EASTERN & CHATHAM /
A225
Polhill Tnl
Shoreham / (Kent)
added (1923)

MAP TWO

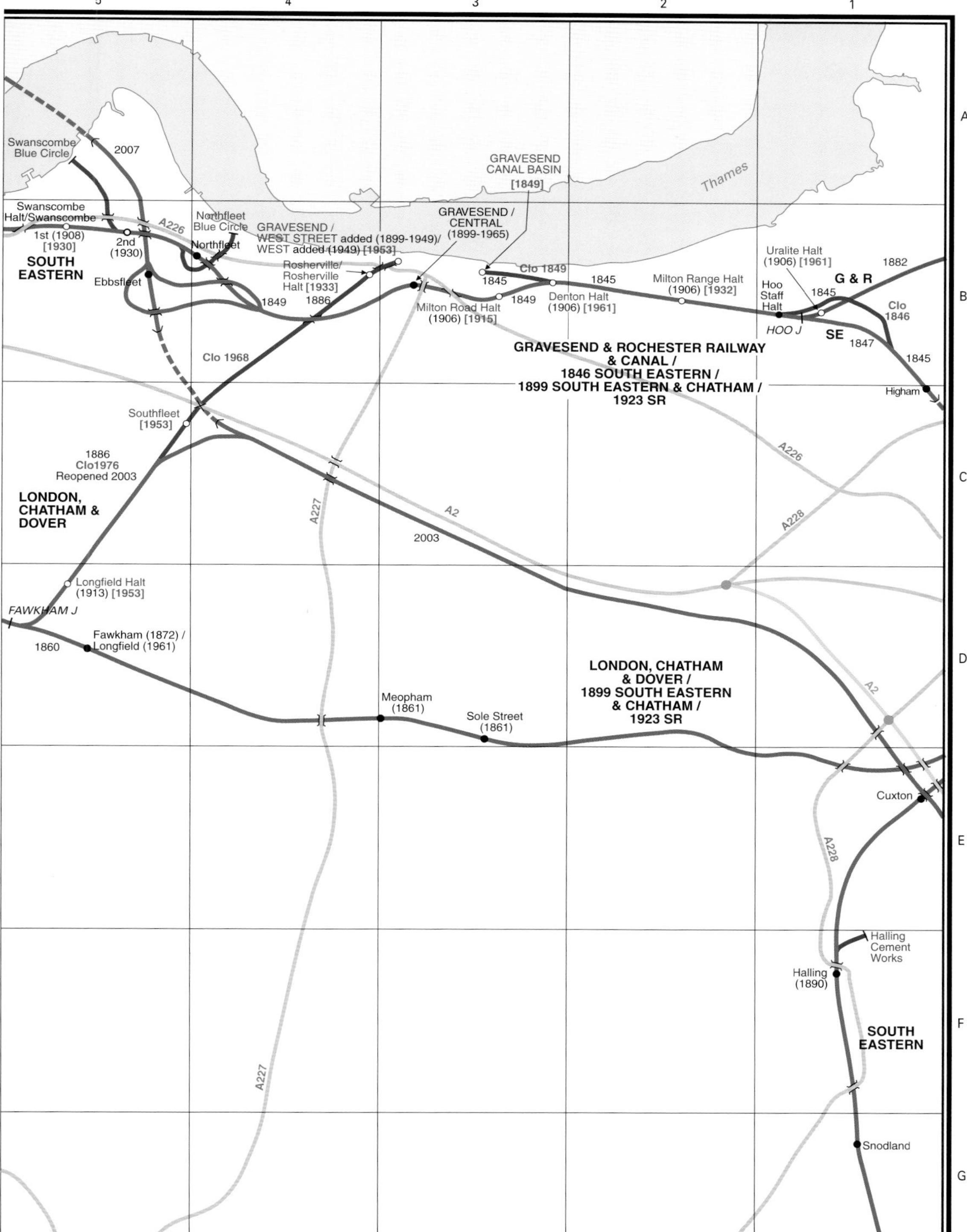

5
4
3
2
1
A
B
C
D
E
F
G
Swanscombe Blue Circle
2007
Thames
GRAVESEND CANAL BASIN [1849]
Swanscombe Halt/Swanscombe 1st (1908) [1930]
2nd (1930)
A226
Northfleet Blue Circle
Northfleet
GRAVESEND / WEST STREET added (1899-1949)/ WEST added (1949) [1953]
GRAVESEND / CENTRAL (1899-1965)
SOUTH EASTERN
Ebbsfleet
Rosherville/ Rosherville Halt [1933]
1849
1886
1845
Clo 1849
1845
Denton Halt (1906) [1961]
Milton Range Halt (1906) [1932]
Uralite Halt (1906) [1961]
1882
G & R
1845
Hoo Staff Halt
Clo 1846
HOO J
SE
1847
1845
Milton Road Halt (1906) [1915]
1849
GRAVESEND & ROCHESTER RAILWAY & CANAL / 1846 SOUTH EASTERN / 1899 SOUTH EASTERN & CHATHAM / 1923 SR
Clo 1968
Higham
Southfleet [1953]
A226
1886 Clo1976 Reopened 2003
LONDON, CHATHAM & DOVER
A227
A2
2003
A228
Longfield Halt (1913) [1953]
FAWKHAM J
Fawkham (1872) / Longfield (1961)
1860
LONDON, CHATHAM & DOVER / 1899 SOUTH EASTERN & CHATHAM / 1923 SR
A2
Meopham (1861)
Sole Street (1861)
Cuxton
A228
Halling Cement Works
Halling (1890)
SOUTH EASTERN
A227
Snodland

MAP THREE

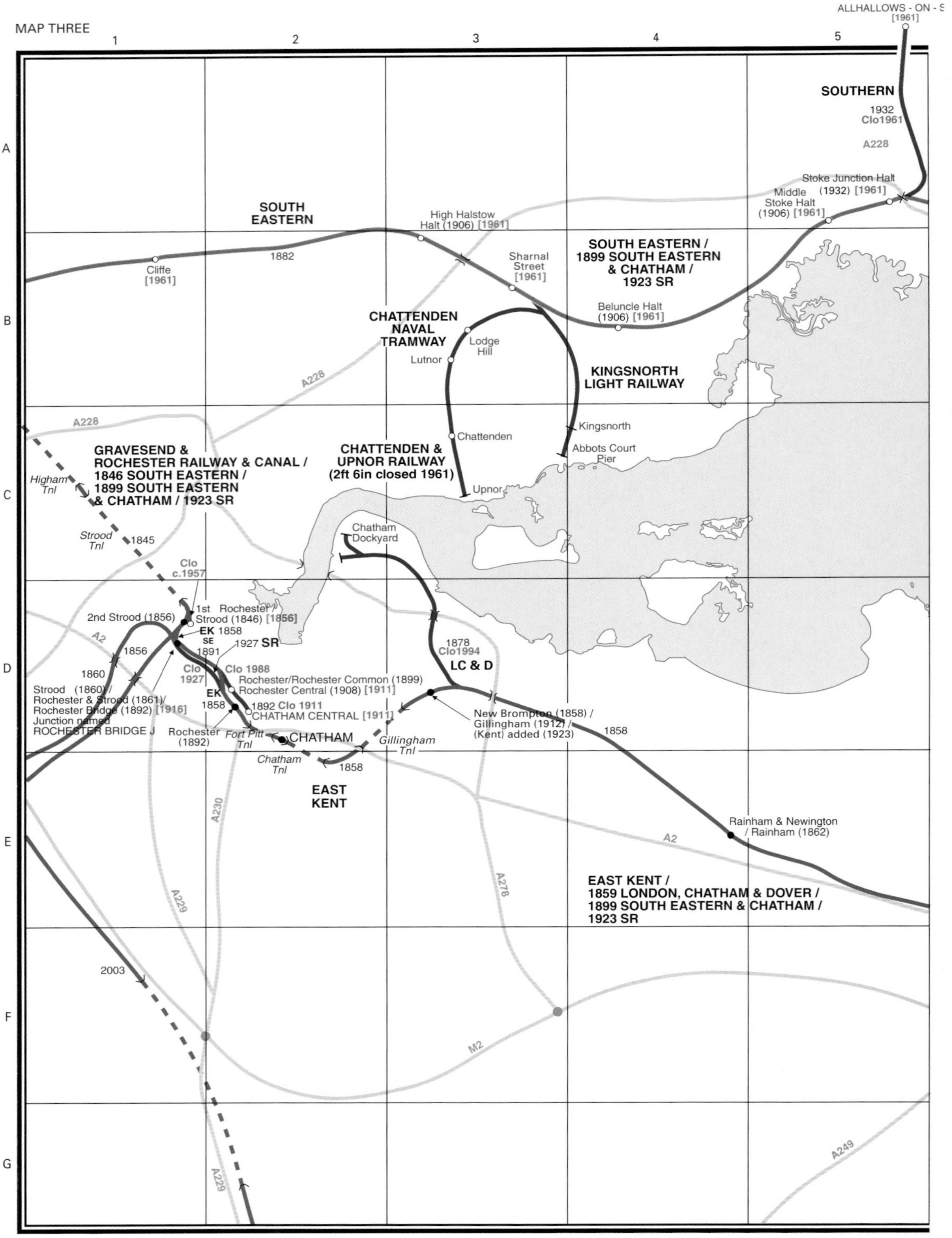

1
2
3
4
5
A
B
C
D
E
F
G
ALLHALLOWS - ON - S
[1961]
SOUTHERN
1932
Clo1961
A228
Stoke Junction Halt
(1932) [1961]
Middle
Stoke Halt
(1906) [1961]
SOUTH
EASTERN
High Halstow
Halt (1906) [1961]
1882
Cliffe
[1961]
Sharnal
Street
[1961]
SOUTH EASTERN /
1899 SOUTH EASTERN
& CHATHAM /
1923 SR
Beluncle Halt
(1906) [1961]
CHATTENDEN
NAVAL
TRAMWAY
Lodge
Hill
Lutnor
KINGSNORTH
LIGHT RAILWAY
A228
A228
Kingsnorth
Chattenden
Abbots Court
Pier
GRAVESEND &
ROCHESTER RAILWAY & CANAL /
1846 SOUTH EASTERN /
1899 SOUTH EASTERN
& CHATHAM / 1923 SR
CHATTENDEN &
UPNOR RAILWAY
(2ft 6in closed 1961)
Higham
Tnl
Upnor
Chatham
Dockyard
Strood
Tnl
1845
Clo
c.1957
1st Rochester /
Strood (1846) [1856]
2nd Strood (1856)
EK 1858
SE
1927 SR
A2
1891
1878
Clo1994
1856
LC & D
Clo
1927
Clo 1988
1860
Rochester/Rochester Common (1899)
Rochester Central (1908) [1911]
Strood (1860) /
Rochester & Strood (1861) /
Rochester Bridge (1892) [1916]
Junction named
ROCHESTER BRIDGE J
EK
1858
1892 Clo 1911
CHATHAM CENTRAL [1911]
New Brompton (1858) /
Gillingham (1912) /
(Kent) added (1923)
1858
Rochester
(1892)
Fort Pitt
Tnl
CHATHAM
Gillingham
Tnl
Chatham
Tnl
1858
EAST
KENT
A230
Rainham & Newington
/ Rainham (1862)
A2
A229
A278
EAST KENT /
1859 LONDON, CHATHAM & DOVER /
1899 SOUTH EASTERN & CHATHAM /
1923 SR
2003
M2
A249
A229

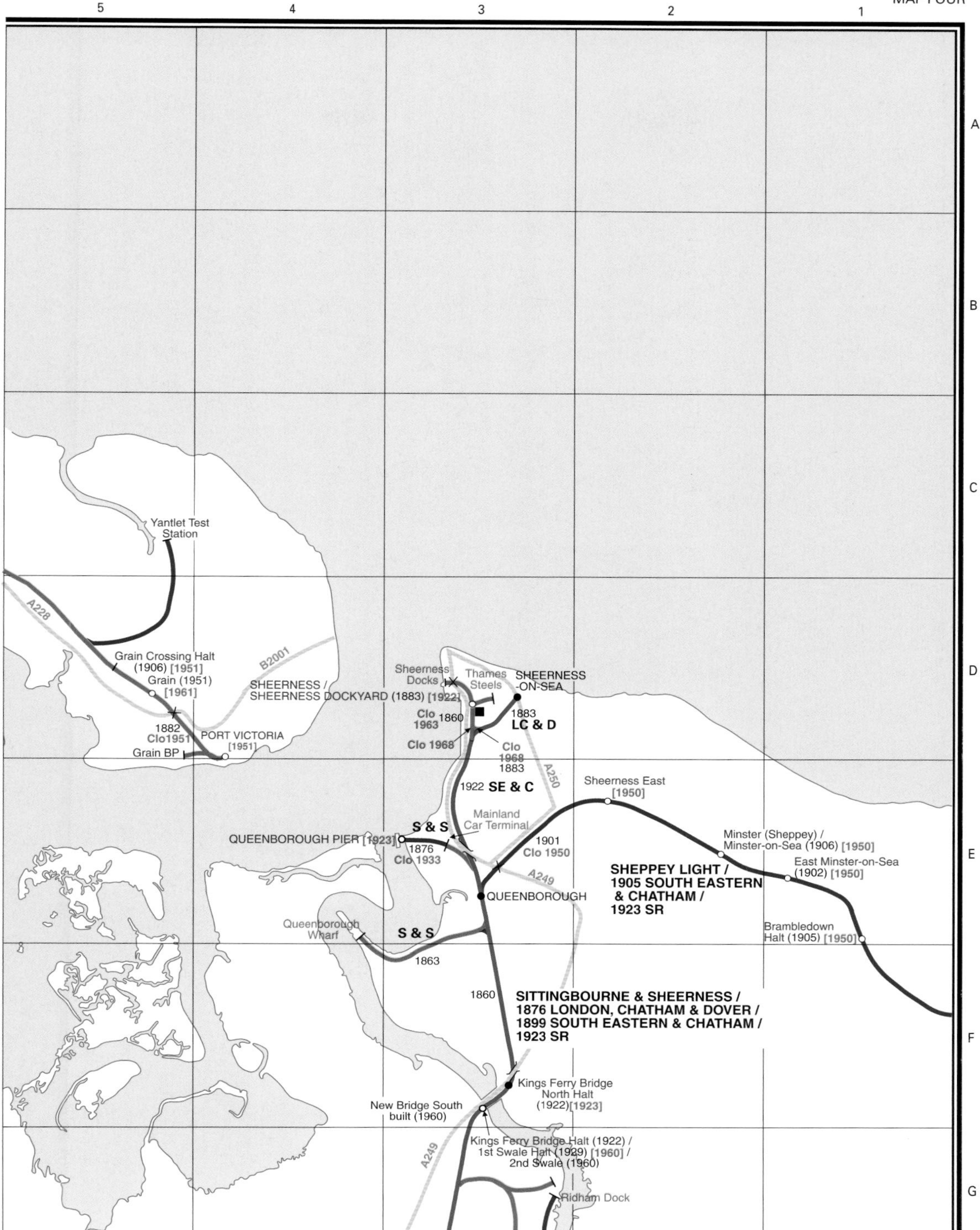

5
4
3
2
1
A
B
C
D
E
F
G
Yantlet Test Station
A228
Grain Crossing Halt (1906) [1951]
Grain (1951) [1961]
B2001
1882
Clo1951
PORT VICTORIA [1951]
Grain BP
SHEERNESS / SHEERNESS DOCKYARD (1883) [1922]
Sheerness Docks
Thames Steels
SHEERNESS -ON-SEA
Clo 1963
1860
1883
LC & D
Clo 1968
Clo 1968
1883
1922
SE & C
A250
Sheerness East [1950]
Mainland Car Terminal
S & S
QUEENBOROUGH PIER [1923]
1876
Clo 1933
1901
Clo 1950
A249
Minster (Sheppey) / Minster-on-Sea (1906) [1950]
East Minster-on-Sea (1902) [1950]
SHEPPEY LIGHT / 1905 SOUTH EASTERN & CHATHAM / 1923 SR
QUEENBOROUGH
Queenborough Wharf
S & S
1863
Brambledown Halt (1905) [1950]
1860
SITTINGBOURNE & SHEERNESS / 1876 LONDON, CHATHAM & DOVER / 1899 SOUTH EASTERN & CHATHAM / 1923 SR
Kings Ferry Bridge North Halt (1922)[1923]
New Bridge South built (1960)
Kings Ferry Bridge Halt (1922) / 1st Swale Halt (1929) [1960] / 2nd Swale (1960)
A249
Ridham Dock

MAP FIVE

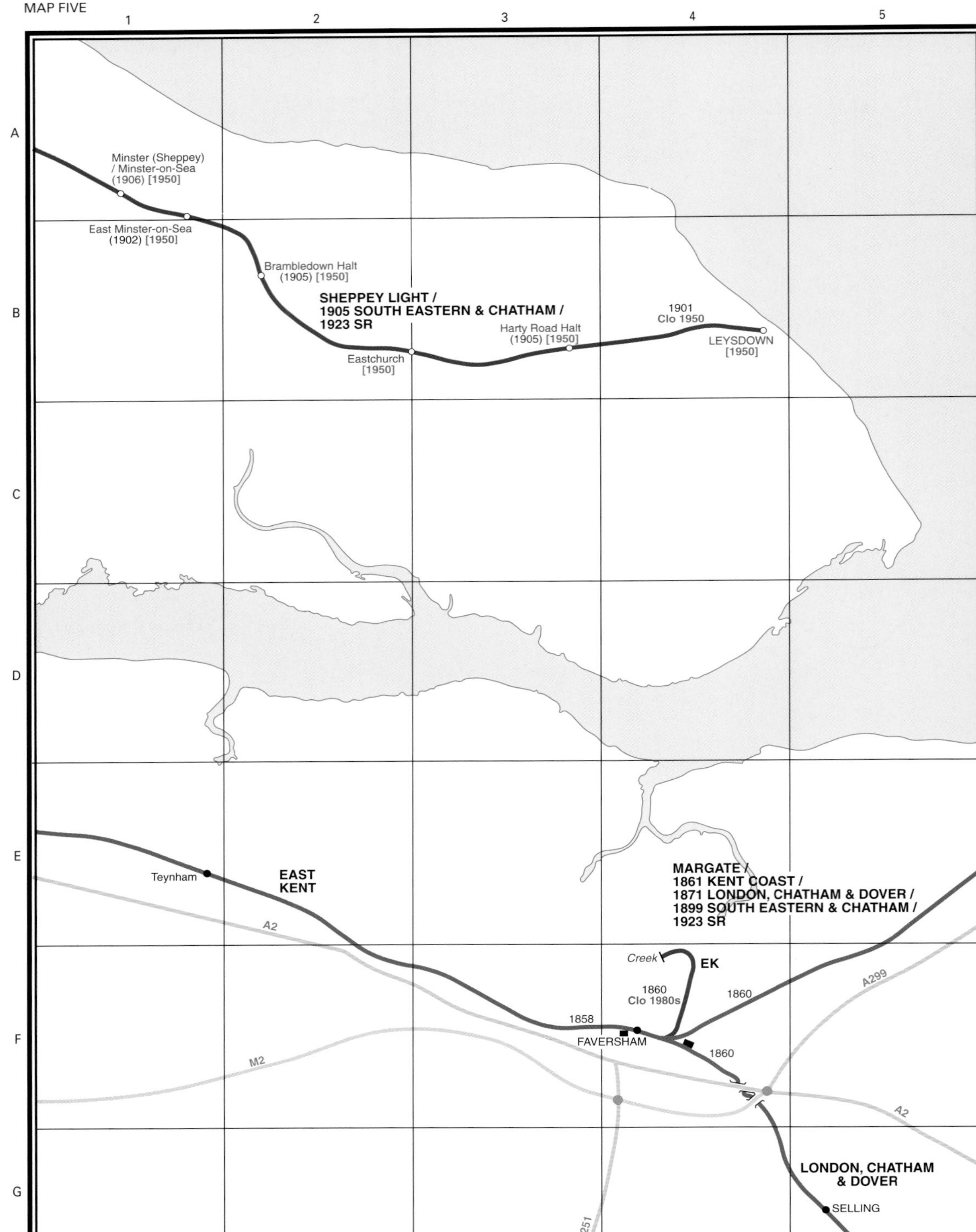
1
2
3
4
5
A
B
C
D
E
F
G
Minster (Sheppey) / Minster-on-Sea (1906) [1950]
East Minster-on-Sea (1902) [1950]
Brambledown Halt (1905) [1950]
SHEPPEY LIGHT / 1905 SOUTH EASTERN & CHATHAM / 1923 SR
Eastchurch [1950]
Harty Road Halt (1905) [1950]
1901 Clo 1950
LEYSDOWN [1950]
Teynham
EAST KENT
A2
MARGATE / 1861 KENT COAST / 1871 LONDON, CHATHAM & DOVER / 1899 SOUTH EASTERN & CHATHAM / 1923 SR
Creek
EK
1860 Clo 1980s
1860
A299
1858
FAVERSHAM
1860
M2
A2
LONDON, CHATHAM & DOVER
SELLING
A251

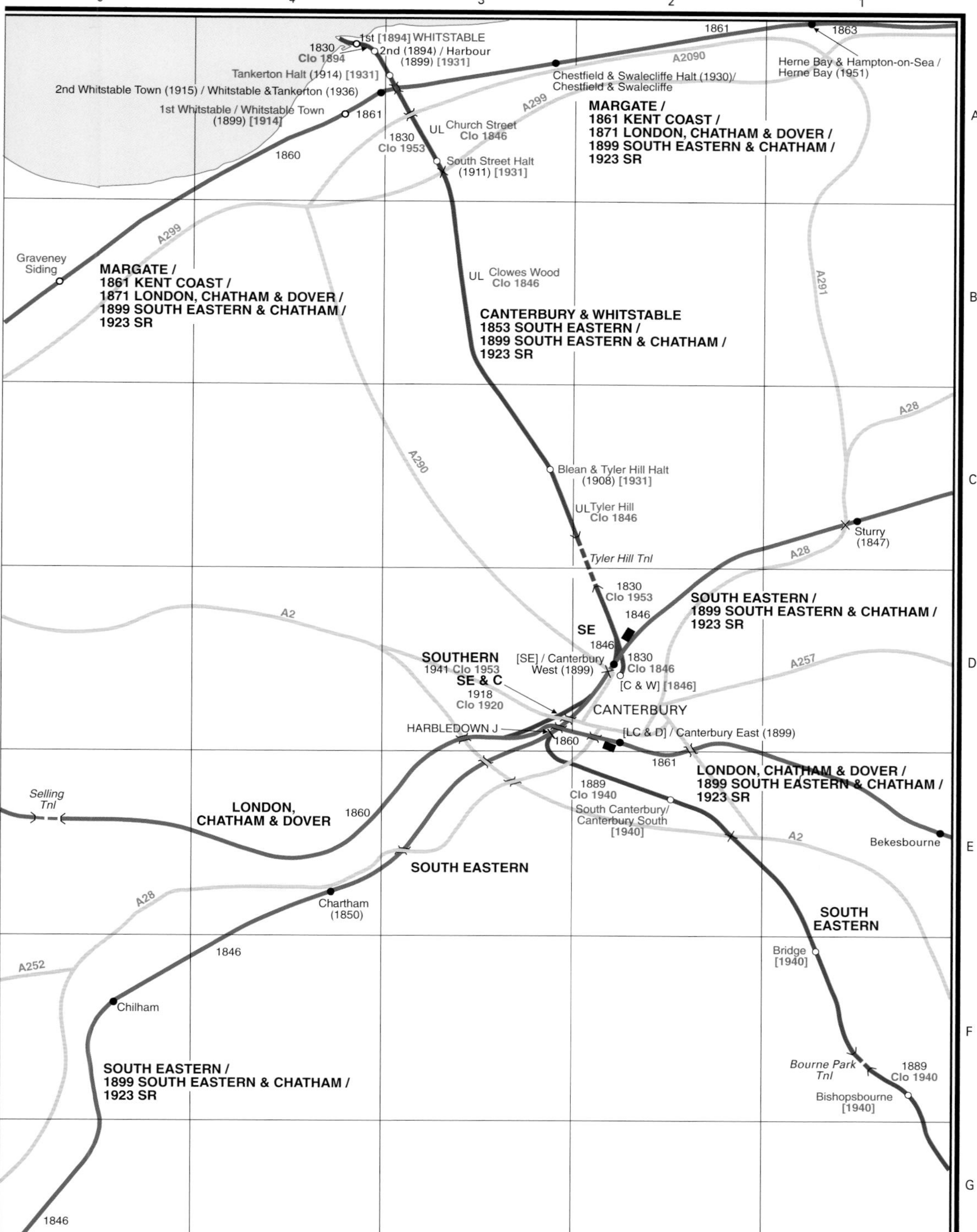

MAP SIX
5
4
3
2
1
A
B
C
D
E
F
G
1st [1894] WHITSTABLE
1830
Clo 1894
2nd (1894) / Harbour
(1899) [1931]
Tankerton Halt (1914) [1931]
2nd Whitstable Town (1915) / Whitstable &Tankerton (1936)
1st Whitstable / Whitstable Town
(1899) [1914]
1861
1860
1861
1863
Herne Bay & Hampton-on-Sea /
Herne Bay (1951)
A2090
Chestfield & Swalecliffe Halt (1930)/
Chestfield & Swalecliffe
A299
MARGATE /
1861 KENT COAST /
1871 LONDON, CHATHAM & DOVER /
1899 SOUTH EASTERN & CHATHAM /
1923 SR
UL
Church Street
Clo 1846
1830
Clo 1953
South Street Halt
(1911) [1931]
Graveney
Siding
A299
MARGATE /
1861 KENT COAST /
1871 LONDON, CHATHAM & DOVER /
1899 SOUTH EASTERN & CHATHAM /
1923 SR
UL
Clowes Wood
Clo 1846
CANTERBURY & WHITSTABLE
1853 SOUTH EASTERN /
1899 SOUTH EASTERN & CHATHAM /
1923 SR
A291
A28
A290
Blean & Tyler Hill Halt
(1908) [1931]
UL
Tyler Hill
Clo 1846
Sturry
(1847)
A28
Tyler Hill Tnl
1830
Clo 1953
SOUTH EASTERN /
1899 SOUTH EASTERN & CHATHAM /
1923 SR
A2
SE
1846
1846
SOUTHERN
1941 Clo 1953
[SE] / Canterbury
West (1899)
1830
Clo 1846
[C & W] [1846]
A257
SE & C
1918
Clo 1920
CANTERBURY
HARBLEDOWN J
1860
[LC & D] / Canterbury East (1899)
1861
LONDON, CHATHAM & DOVER /
1899 SOUTH EASTERN & CHATHAM /
1923 SR
Selling
Tnl
LONDON,
CHATHAM & DOVER
1860
1889
Clo 1940
South Canterbury/
Canterbury South
[1940]
A2
Bekesbourne
SOUTH EASTERN
A28
Chartham
(1850)
SOUTH
EASTERN
A252
1846
Bridge
[1940]
Chilham
Bourne Park
Tnl
1889
Clo 1940
SOUTH EASTERN /
1899 SOUTH EASTERN & CHATHAM /
1923 SR
Bishopsbourne
[1940]
1846

MAP SEVEN

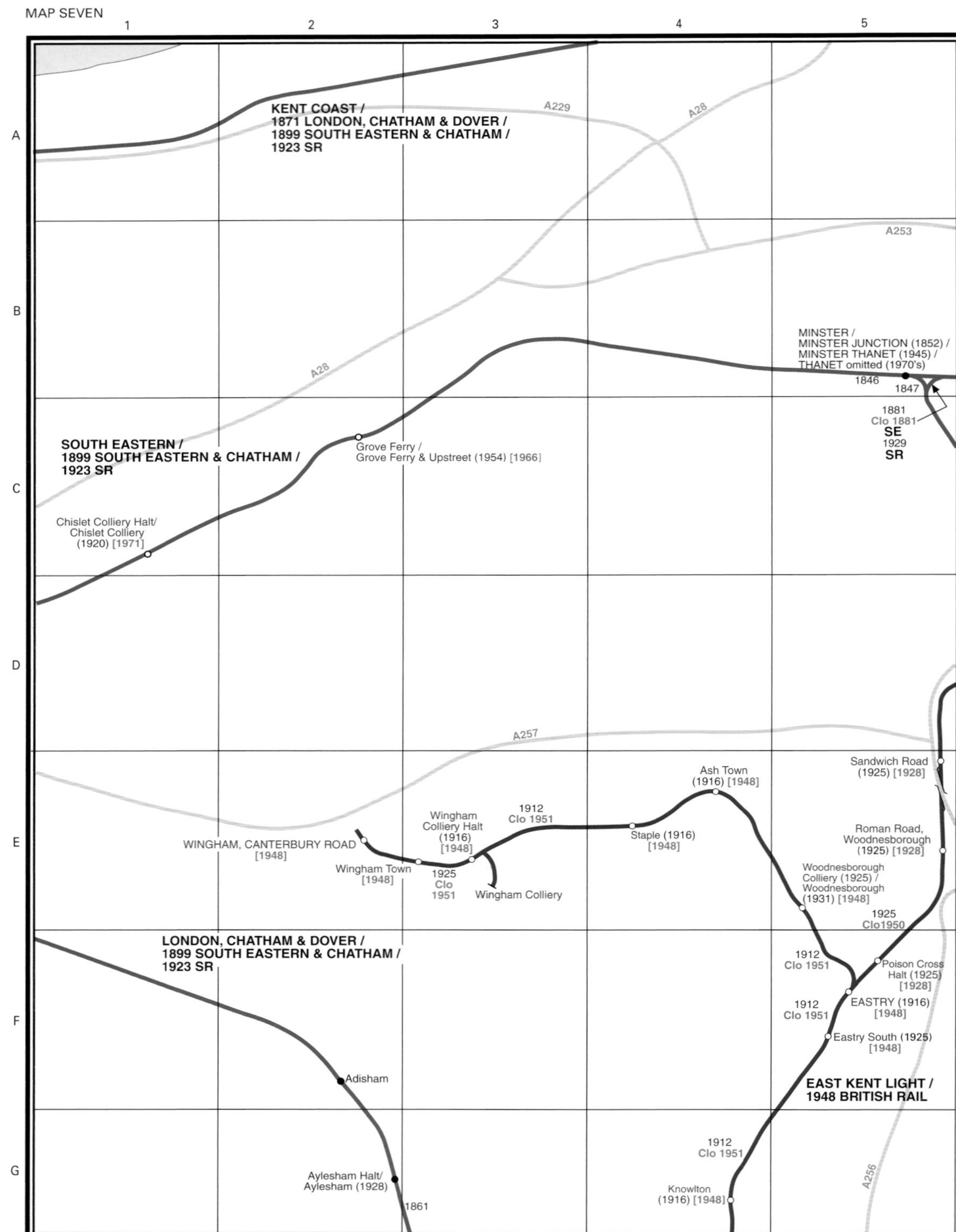
1
2
3
4
5
A
B
C
D
E
F
G
KENT COAST /
1871 LONDON, CHATHAM & DOVER /
1899 SOUTH EASTERN & CHATHAM /
1923 SR
A229
A28
A253
A28
MINSTER /
MINSTER JUNCTION (1852) /
MINSTER THANET (1945) /
THANET omitted (1970's)
1846
1847
1881
Clo 1881
SE
1929
SR
SOUTH EASTERN /
1899 SOUTH EASTERN & CHATHAM /
1923 SR
Grove Ferry /
Grove Ferry & Upstreet (1954) [1966]
Chislet Colliery Halt/
Chislet Colliery
(1920) [1971]
A257
Sandwich Road
(1925) [1928]
Ash Town
(1916) [1948]
1912
Clo 1951
Wingham
Colliery Halt
(1916)
[1948]
Staple (1916)
[1948]
WINGHAM, CANTERBURY ROAD
[1948]
Roman Road,
Woodnesborough
(1925) [1928]
Wingham Town
[1948]
1925
Clo
1951
Wingham Colliery
Woodnesborough
Colliery (1925) /
Woodnesborough
(1931) [1948]
1925
Clo1950
LONDON, CHATHAM & DOVER /
1899 SOUTH EASTERN & CHATHAM /
1923 SR
1912
Clo 1951
Poison Cross
Halt (1925)
[1928]
EASTRY (1916)
[1948]
1912
Clo 1951
Eastry South (1925)
[1948]
Adisham
EAST KENT LIGHT /
1948 BRITISH RAIL
1912
Clo 1951
Aylesham Halt/
Aylesham (1928)
1861
Knowlton
(1916) [1948]
A256

MAP EIGHT

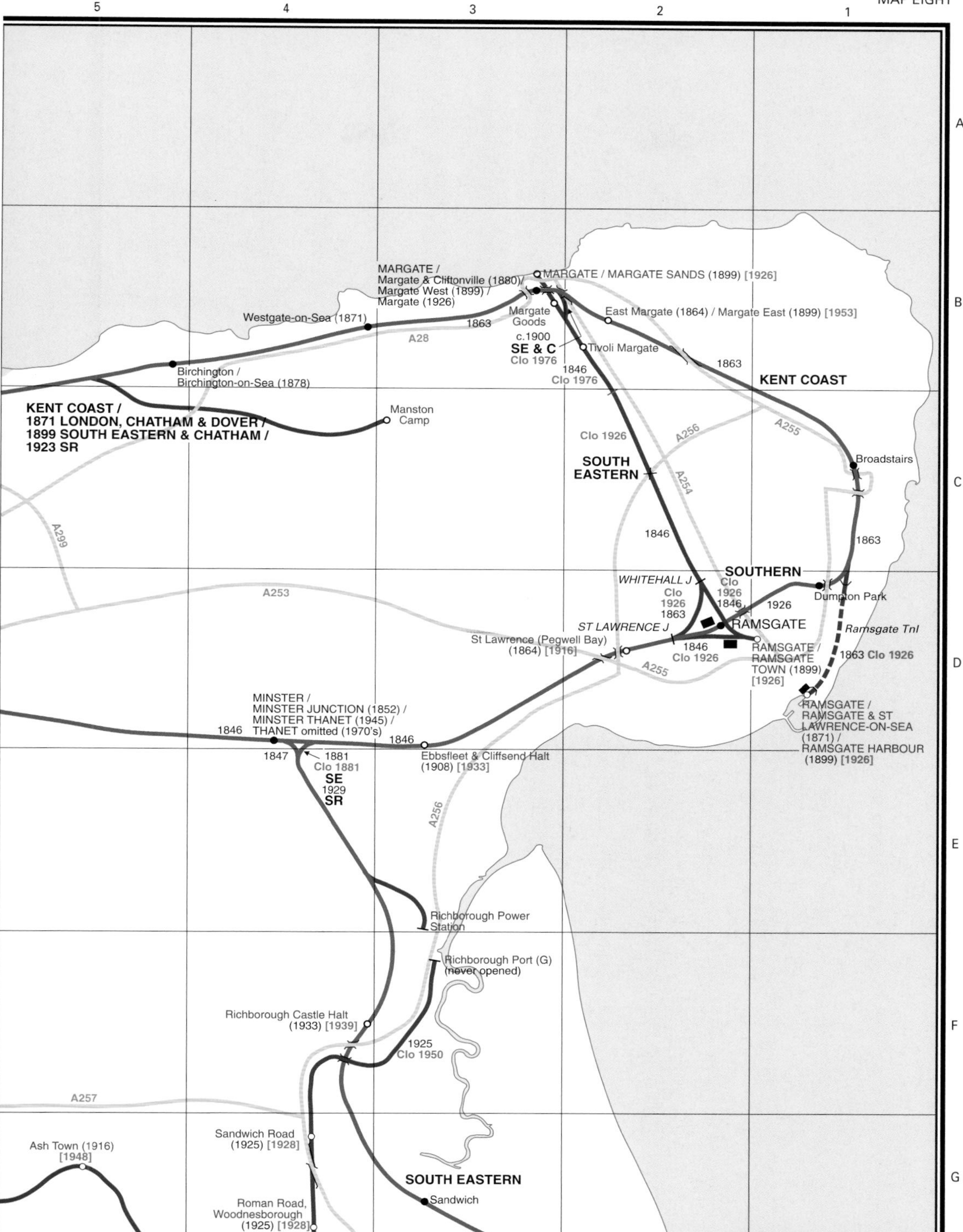

5
4
3
2
1
A
B
C
D
E
F
G
MARGATE / MARGATE SANDS (1899) [1926]
MARGATE /
Margate & Cliftonville (1880) /
Margate West (1899) /
Margate (1926)
Margate Goods
c.1900
SE & C
Clo 1976
Tivoli Margate
1846
Clo 1976
East Margate (1864) / Margate East (1899) [1953]
Westgate-on-Sea (1871)
1863
A28
Birchington /
Birchington-on-Sea (1878)
1863
KENT COAST
KENT COAST /
1871 LONDON, CHATHAM & DOVER /
1899 SOUTH EASTERN & CHATHAM /
1923 SR
Manston Camp
Clo 1926
A256
A255
Broadstairs
SOUTH EASTERN
A254
A299
1846
1863
SOUTHERN
WHITEHALL J
Clo
1926
1846
Clo
1926
1863
1926
Dumpton Park
A253
ST LAWRENCE J
RAMSGATE
Ramsgate Tnl
St Lawrence (Pegwell Bay)
(1864) [1916]
1846
Clo 1926
RAMSGATE /
RAMSGATE
TOWN (1899)
[1926]
1863 Clo 1926
A255
MINSTER /
MINSTER JUNCTION (1852) /
MINSTER THANET (1945) /
THANET omitted (1970's)
1846
1846
RAMSGATE /
RAMSGATE & ST
LAWRENCE-ON-SEA
(1871) /
RAMSGATE HARBOUR
(1899) [1926]
1847
1881
Clo 1881
SE
1929
SR
Ebbsfleet & Cliffsend Halt
(1908) [1933]
A256
Richborough Power
Station
Richborough Port (G)
(never opened)
Richborough Castle Halt
(1933) [1939]
1925
Clo 1950
A257
Sandwich Road
(1925) [1928]
Ash Town (1916)
[1948]
SOUTH EASTERN
Sandwich
Roman Road,
Woodnesborough
(1925) [1928]

MAP NINE

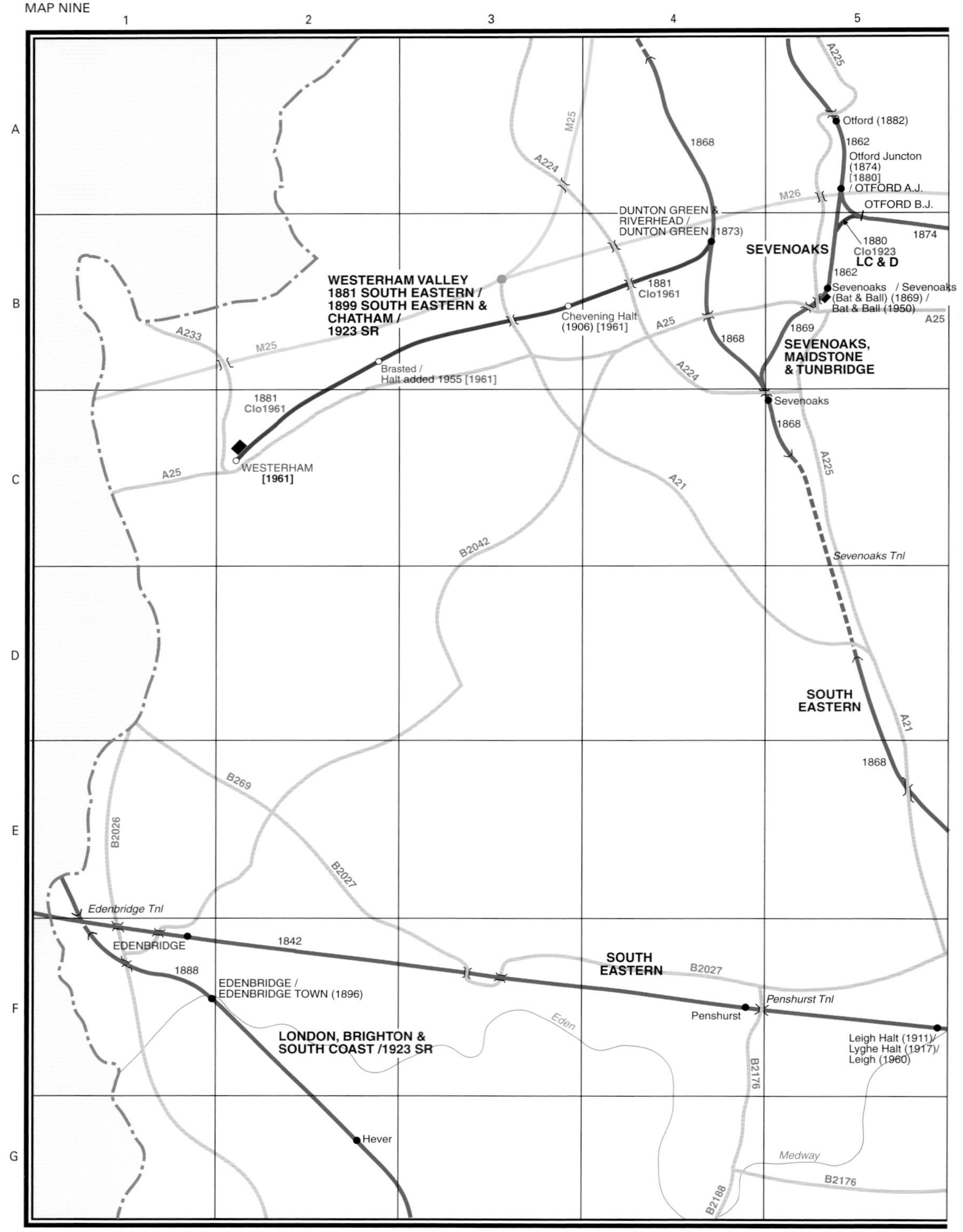

1 2 3 4 5

A B C D E F G

A225
Otford (1882)
1862
Otford Juncton
(1874)
[1880]
/ OTFORD A.J.
OTFORD B.J.
1880
Clo1923
1874
M25
1868
A224
M26
DUNTON GREEN &
RIVERHEAD /
DUNTON GREEN (1873)
SEVENOAKS
LC & D
1862
Sevenoaks / Sevenoaks
(Bat & Ball) (1869) /
Bat & Ball (1950)
A25
WESTERHAM VALLEY
1881 SOUTH EASTERN /
1899 SOUTH EASTERN &
CHATHAM /
1923 SR
1881
Clo1961
Chevening Halt
(1906) [1961]
A25
1868
1869
SEVENOAKS,
MAIDSTONE
& TUNBRIDGE
A233
M25
Brasted /
Halt added 1955 [1961]
A224
Sevenoaks
1881
Clo1961
1868
WESTERHAM
[1961]
A25
A21
A225
B2042
Sevenoaks Tnl
SOUTH
EASTERN
A21
1868
B269
B2026
B2027
Edenbridge Tnl
EDENBRIDGE
1842
SOUTH
EASTERN
B2027
1888
EDENBRIDGE /
EDENBRIDGE TOWN (1896)
Penshurst
Penshurst Tnl
Eden
LONDON, BRIGHTON &
SOUTH COAST /1923 SR
B2176
Leigh Halt (1911)/
Lyghe Halt (1917)/
Leigh (1960)
Hever
Medway
B2176
B2188

MAP TEN

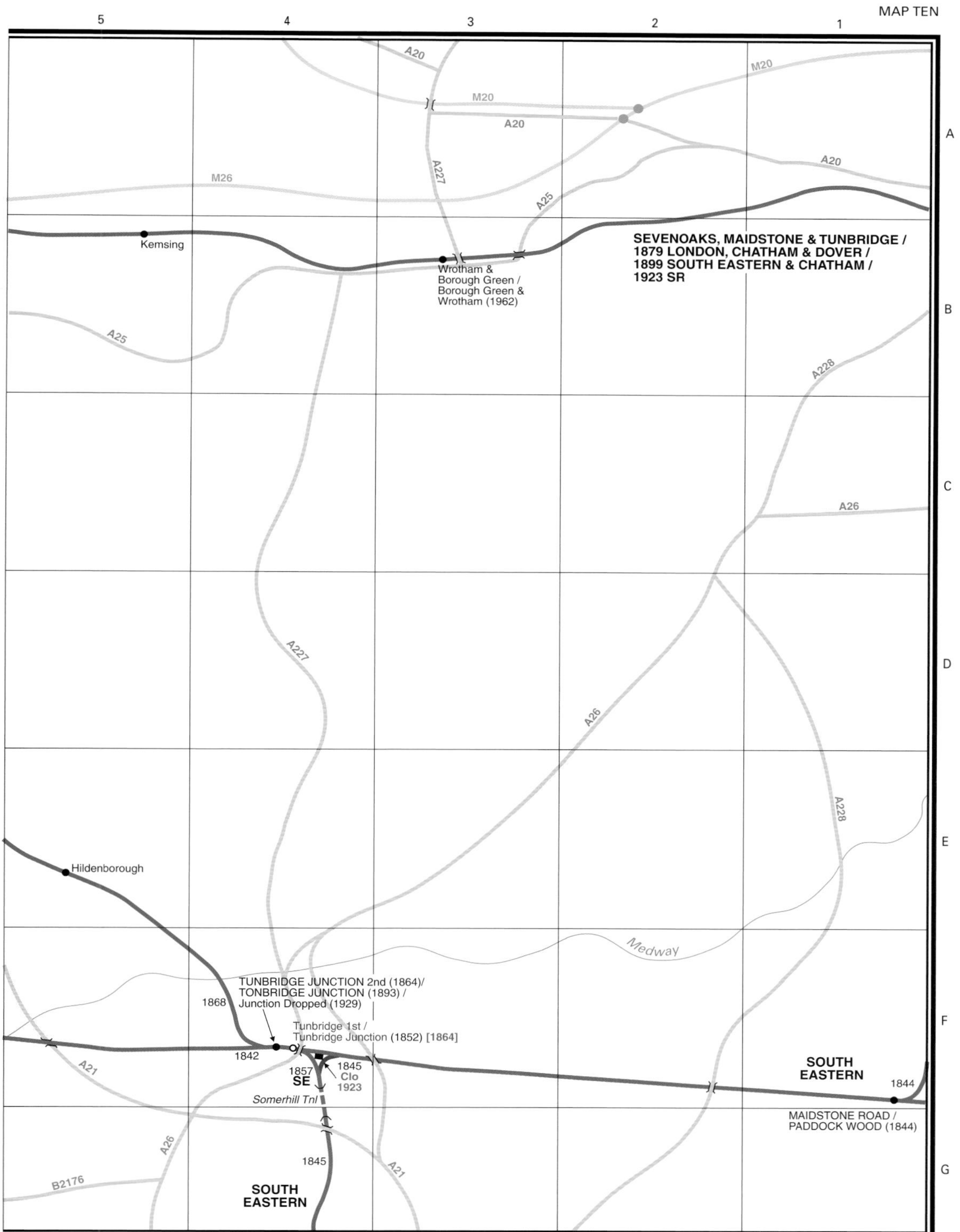
5
4
3
2
1
A
B
C
D
E
F
G
A20
M20
M20
A20
A20
A227
M26
A25
Kemsing
Wrotham &
Borough Green /
Borough Green &
Wrotham (1962)
SEVENOAKS, MAIDSTONE & TUNBRIDGE /
1879 LONDON, CHATHAM & DOVER /
1899 SOUTH EASTERN & CHATHAM /
1923 SR
A25
A228
A26
A227
A26
A228
Hildenborough
Medway
TUNBRIDGE JUNCTION 2nd (1864)/
TONBRIDGE JUNCTION (1893) /
Junction Dropped (1929)
1868
Tunbridge 1st /
Tunbridge Junction (1852) [1864]
1842
A21
1857
SE
1845
Clo
1923
Somerhill Tnl
SOUTH
EASTERN
1844
MAIDSTONE ROAD /
PADDOCK WOOD (1844)
A26
1845
A21
B2176
SOUTH
EASTERN

MAP ELEVEN

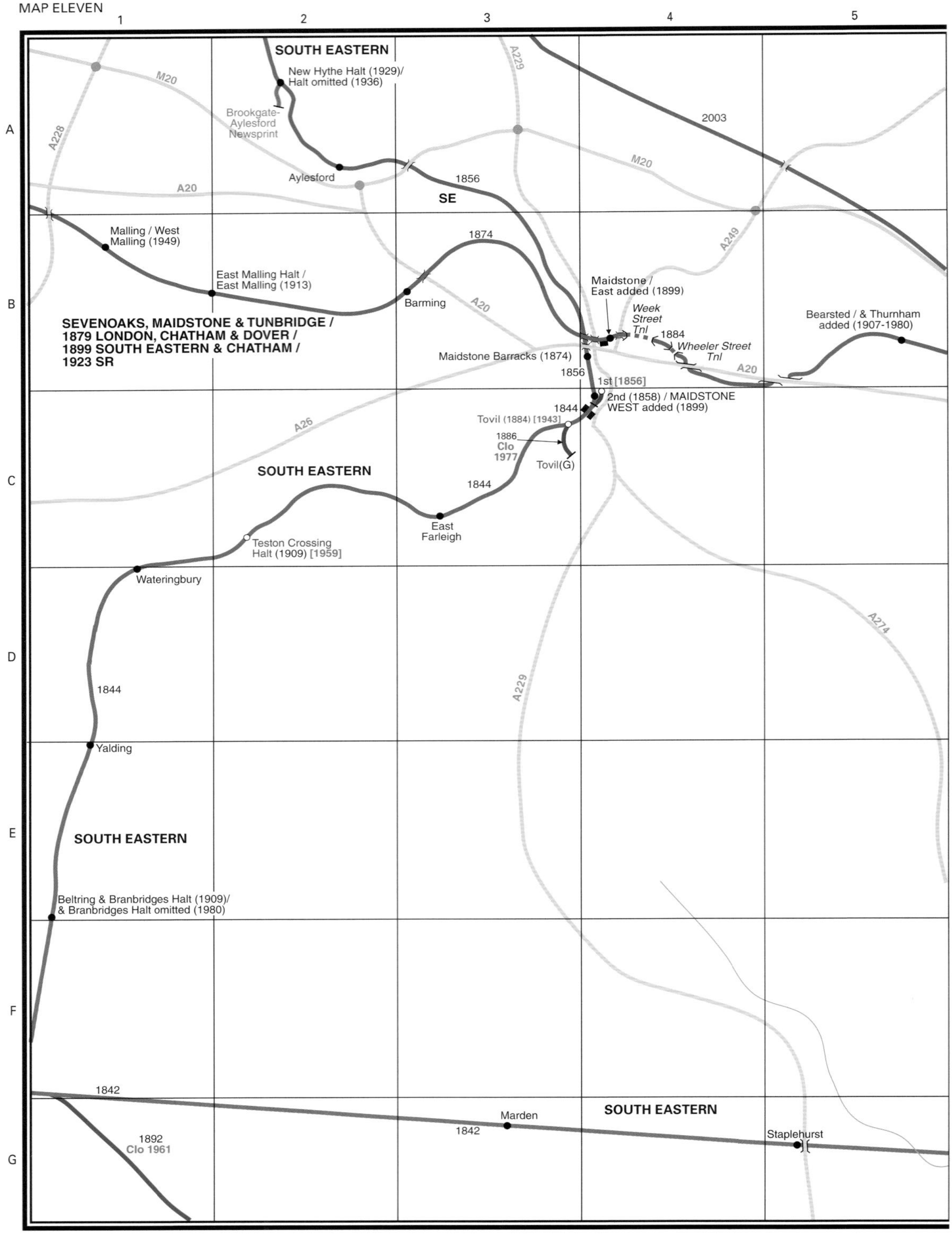

1 2 3 4 5

A B C D E F G

SOUTH EASTERN

New Hythe Halt (1929)/
Halt omitted (1936)

Brookgate-
Aylesford
Newsprint

Aylesford

1856

SE

2003

M20

A228

A20

A229

A249

Malling / West
Malling (1949)

East Malling Halt /
East Malling (1913)

1874

Barming

SEVENOAKS, MAIDSTONE & TUNBRIDGE /
1879 LONDON, CHATHAM & DOVER /
1899 SOUTH EASTERN & CHATHAM /
1923 SR

Maidstone /
East added (1899)

Week
Street
Tnl

1884

Wheeler Street
Tnl

Bearsted / & Thurnham
added (1907-1980)

Maidstone Barracks (1874)

1856

1st [1856]

2nd (1858) / MAIDSTONE
WEST added (1899)

1844

Tovil (1884) [1943]

1886
Clo
1977

Tovil(G)

A26

SOUTH EASTERN

1844

East
Farleigh

Teston Crossing
Halt (1909) [1959]

Wateringbury

A274

1844

Yalding

SOUTH EASTERN

Beltring & Branbridges Halt (1909)/
& Branbridges Halt omitted (1980)

1842

Marden

1842

SOUTH EASTERN

Staplehurst

1892
Clo 1961

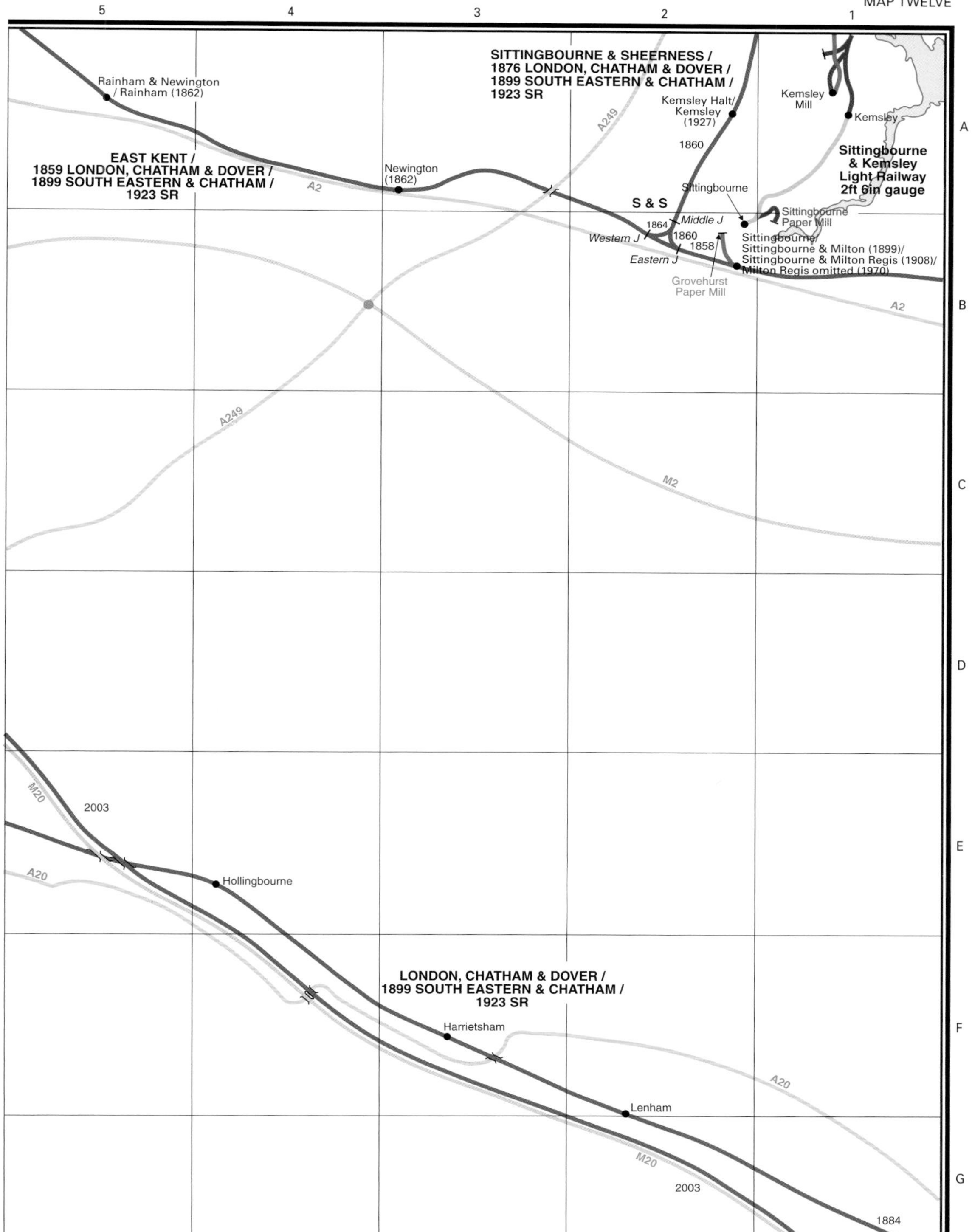
5
4
3
2
1
A
B
C
D
E
F
G
Rainham & Newington / Rainham (1862)
EAST KENT / 1859 LONDON, CHATHAM & DOVER / 1899 SOUTH EASTERN & CHATHAM / 1923 SR
A2
Newington (1862)
SITTINGBOURNE & SHEERNESS / 1876 LONDON, CHATHAM & DOVER / 1899 SOUTH EASTERN & CHATHAM / 1923 SR
A249
Kemsley Halt/ Kemsley (1927)
Kemsley Mill
Kemsley
1860
Sittingbourne & Kemsley Light Railway 2ft 6in gauge
Sittingbourne
S & S
Sittingbourne Paper Mill
Middle J
1864
Western J
1860
1858
Eastern J
Sittingbourne/ Sittingbourne & Milton (1899)/ Sittingbourne & Milton Regis (1908)/ Milton Regis omitted (1970)
Grovehurst Paper Mill
A2
A249
M2
M20
2003
A20
Hollingbourne
LONDON, CHATHAM & DOVER / 1899 SOUTH EASTERN & CHATHAM / 1923 SR
Harrietsham
A20
Lenham
M20
2003
1884

MAP THIRTEEN

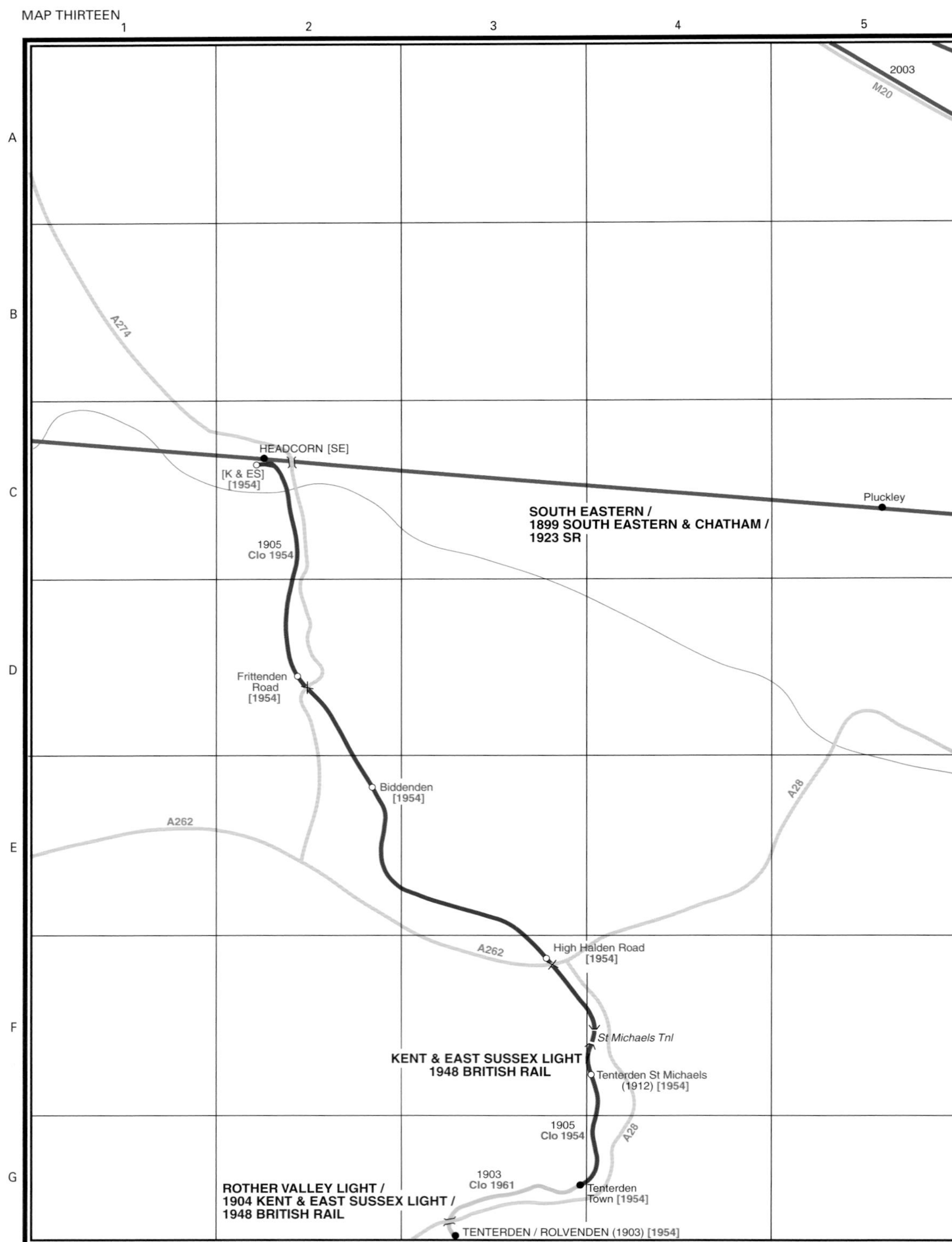

1
2
3
4
5
A
B
C
D
E
F
G
2003
M20
A274
HEADCORN [SE]
[K & ES]
[1954]
Pluckley
SOUTH EASTERN /
1899 SOUTH EASTERN & CHATHAM /
1923 SR
1905
Clo 1954
Frittenden
Road
[1954]
Biddenden
[1954]
A262
A28
A262
High Halden Road
[1954]
St Michaels Tnl
KENT & EAST SUSSEX LIGHT /
1948 BRITISH RAIL
Tenterden St Michaels
(1912) [1954]
1905
Clo 1954
A28
1903
Clo 1961
Tenterden
Town [1954]
ROTHER VALLEY LIGHT /
1904 KENT & EAST SUSSEX LIGHT /
1948 BRITISH RAIL
TENTERDEN / ROLVENDEN (1903) [1954]

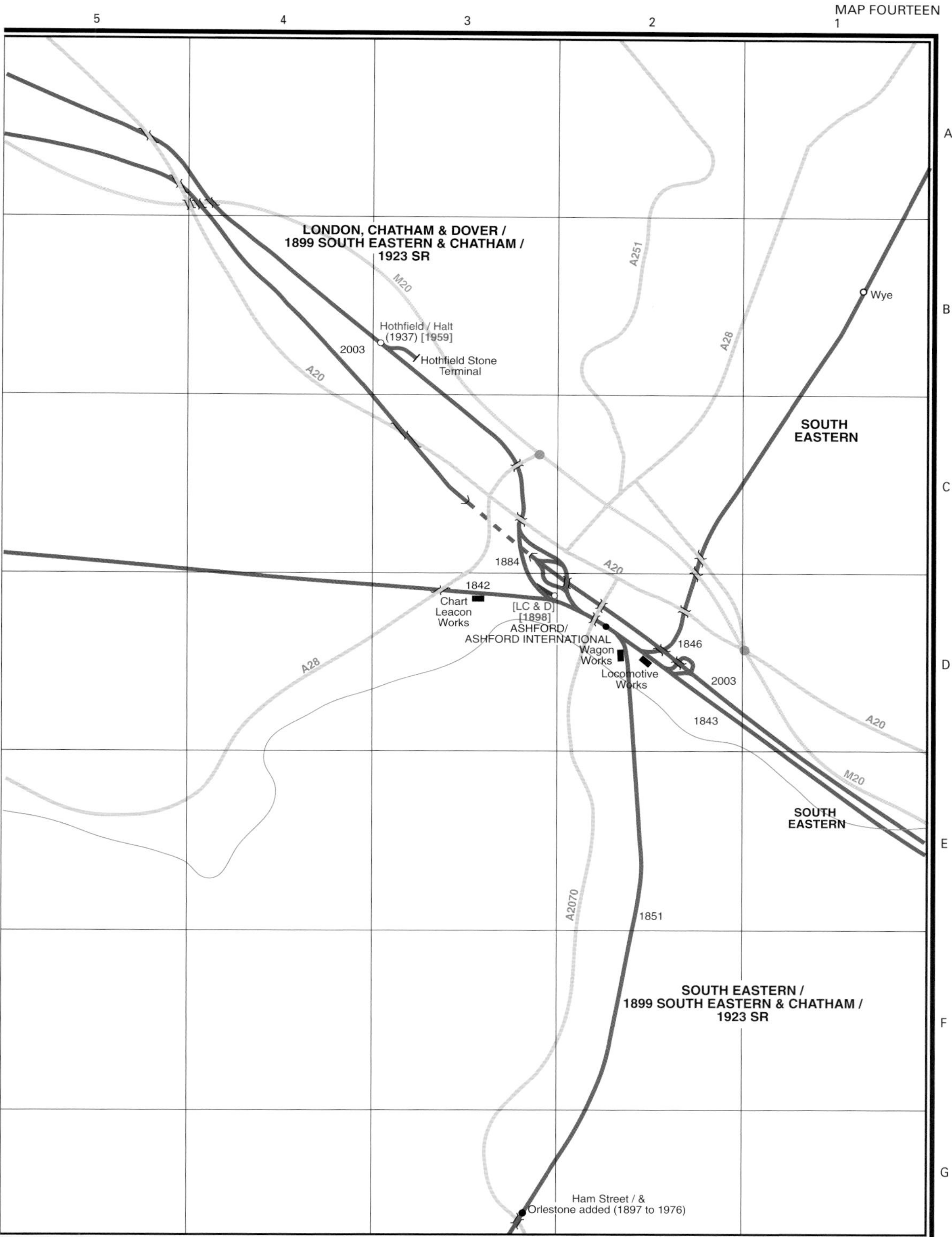

MAP FOURTEEN
5
4
3
2
1
A
B
C
D
E
F
G
LONDON, CHATHAM & DOVER /
1899 SOUTH EASTERN & CHATHAM /
1923 SR
M20
A251
A28
A20
Wye
Hothfield / Halt
(1937) [1959]
2003
Hothfield Stone
Terminal
SOUTH
EASTERN
1884
1842
Chart
Leacon
Works
[LC & D]
[1898]
ASHFORD/
ASHFORD INTERNATIONAL
Wagon
Works
Locomotive
Works
1846
2003
1843
SOUTH
EASTERN
A2070
1851
SOUTH EASTERN /
1899 SOUTH EASTERN & CHATHAM /
1923 SR
Ham Street / &
Orlestone added (1897 to 1976)

MAP FIFTEEN

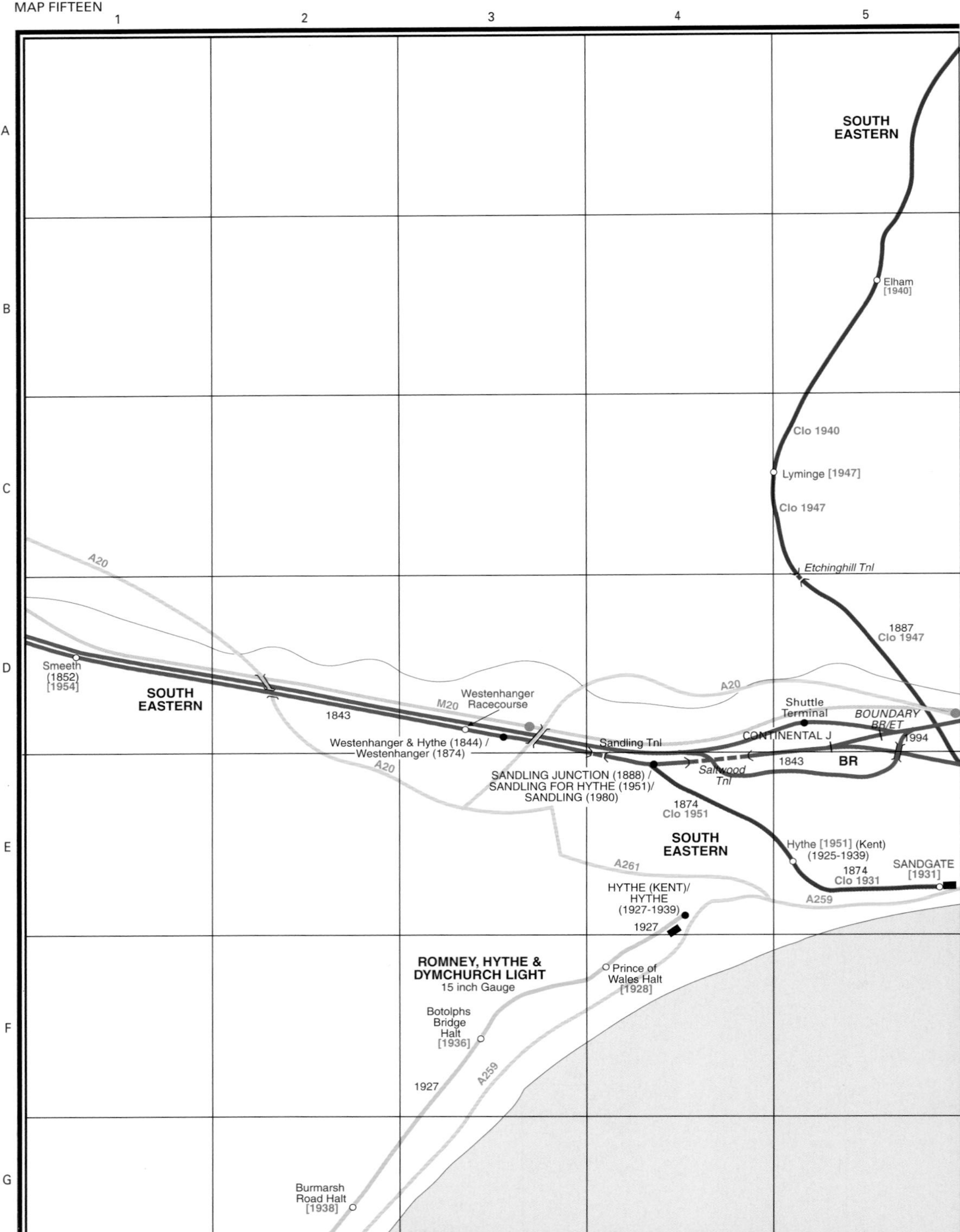
1
2
3
4
5
A
B
C
D
E
F
G
SOUTH EASTERN
Elham [1940]
Clo 1940
Lyminge [1947]
Clo 1947
Etchinghill Tnl
1887
Clo 1947
A20
Smeeth (1852) [1954]
SOUTH EASTERN
1843
M20
Westenhanger Racecourse
Westenhanger & Hythe (1844) / Westenhanger (1874)
A20
Sandling Tnl
A20
Shuttle Terminal
BOUNDARY BR/ET
CONTINENTAL J
1994
1843
BR
Saltwood Tnl
SANDLING JUNCTION (1888) / SANDLING FOR HYTHE (1951)/ SANDLING (1980)
1874
Clo 1951
SOUTH EASTERN
Hythe [1951] (Kent) (1925-1939)
1874
Clo 1931
SANDGATE [1931]
A261
A259
HYTHE (KENT)/ HYTHE (1927-1939)
1927
ROMNEY, HYTHE & DYMCHURCH LIGHT
15 inch Gauge
Prince of Wales Halt [1928]
Botolphs Bridge Halt [1936]
A259
1927
Burmarsh Road Halt [1938]

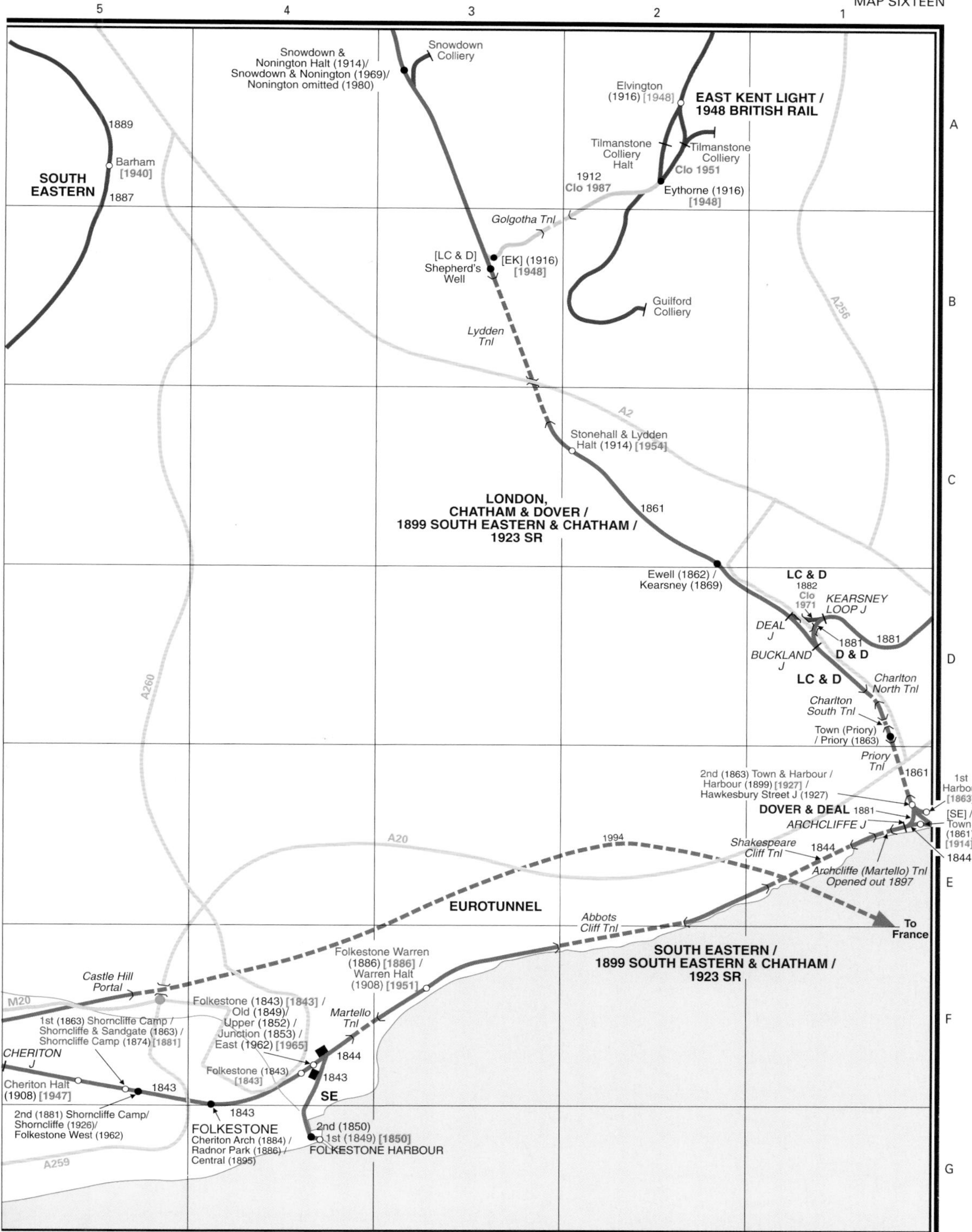

5
4
3
2
1
A
B
C
D
E
F
G
SOUTH EASTERN
1889
Barham [1940]
1887
Snowdown & Nonington Halt (1914)/ Snowdown & Nonington (1969)/ Nonington omitted (1980)
Snowdown Colliery
Elvington (1916) [1948]
EAST KENT LIGHT / 1948 BRITISH RAIL
Tilmanstone Colliery Halt
Tilmanstone Colliery
Clo 1951
1912
Clo 1987
Eythorne (1916) [1948]
Golgotha Tnl
[LC & D] Shepherd's Well
[EK] (1916) [1948]
Guilford Colliery
A256
Lydden Tnl
A2
Stonehall & Lydden Halt (1914) [1954]
LONDON, CHATHAM & DOVER / 1899 SOUTH EASTERN & CHATHAM / 1923 SR
1861
Ewell (1862) / Kearsney (1869)
LC & D
1882
Clo 1971
KEARSNEY LOOP J
DEAL J
1881
1881
BUCKLAND J
D & D
LC & D
Charlton North Tnl
Charlton South Tnl
Town (Priory) / Priory (1863)
Priory Tnl
1861
A260
2nd (1863) Town & Harbour / Harbour (1899) [1927] / Hawkesbury Street J (1927)
1st Harbou [1863]
DOVER & DEAL 1881
[SE] / Town (1861) [1914]
ARCHCLIFFE J
A20
1994
Shakespeare Cliff Tnl
1844
1844
Archcliffe (Martello) Tnl Opened out 1897
EUROTUNNEL
To France
Abbots Cliff Tnl
SOUTH EASTERN / 1899 SOUTH EASTERN & CHATHAM / 1923 SR
Castle Hill Portal
Folkestone Warren (1886) [1886] / Warren Halt (1908) [1951]
M20
Folkestone (1843) [1843] / Old (1849)/ Upper (1852) / Junction (1853) / East (1962) [1965]
Martello Tnl
1st (1863) Shorncliffe Camp / Shorncliffe & Sandgate (1863) / Shorncliffe Camp (1874) [1881]
CHERITON J
1844
Folkestone (1843) [1843]
1843
Cheriton Halt (1908) [1947]
1843
SE
1843
2nd (1881) Shorncliffe Camp/ Shorncliffe (1926)/ Folkestone West (1962)
FOLKESTONE
Cheriton Arch (1884) / Radnor Park (1886) / Central (1895)
2nd (1850)
1st (1849) [1850]
FOLKESTONE HARBOUR
A259

MAP SEVENTEEN

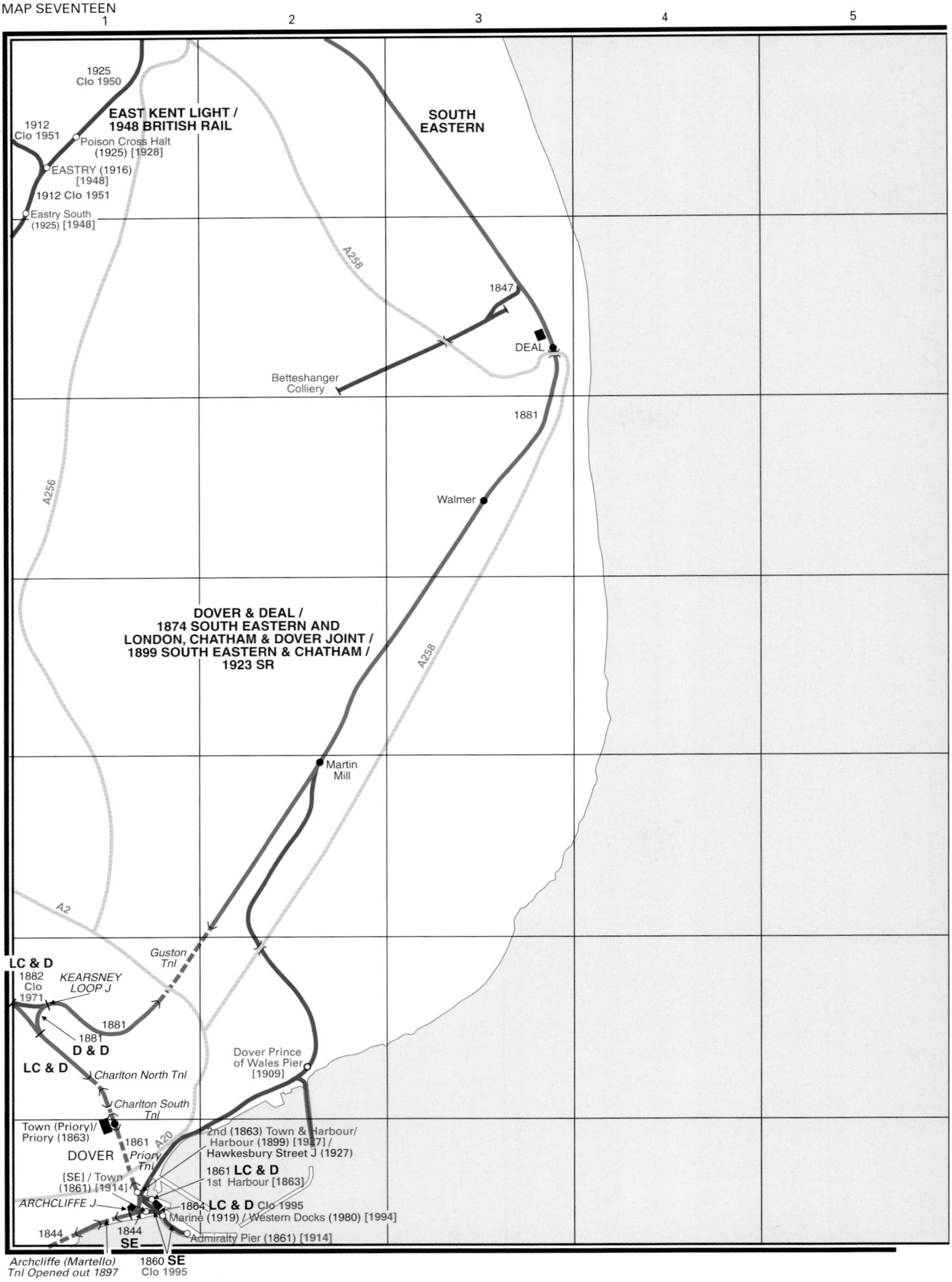

1 2 3 4 5

A B C D E F G

1925
Clo 1950
EAST KENT LIGHT /
1948 BRITISH RAIL
1912
Clo 1951
Poison Cross Halt
(1925) [1928]
EASTRY (1916)
[1948]
1912 Clo 1951
Eastry South
(1925) [1948]
SOUTH
EASTERN
A258
1847
DEAL
Betteshanger
Colliery
1881
A256
Walmer
DOVER & DEAL /
1874 SOUTH EASTERN AND
LONDON, CHATHAM & DOVER JOINT /
1899 SOUTH EASTERN & CHATHAM /
1923 SR
A258
Martin
Mill
A2
Guston
Tnl
LC & D
1882
Clo
1971
KEARSNEY
LOOP J
1881
1881
D & D
LC & D
Charlton North Tnl
Dover Prince
of Wales Pier
[1909]
Charlton South
Tnl
Town (Priory)/
Priory (1863)
1861
Priory
Tnl
A20
DOVER
2nd (1863) Town & Harbour/
Harbour (1899) [1927] /
Hawkesbury Street J (1927)
1861 LC & D
1st Harbour [1863]
[SE] / Town
(1861) [1914]
ARCHCLIFFE J
1864 LC & D Clo 1995
Marine (1919) / Western Docks (1980) [1994]
1844
1844
SE
Admiralty Pier (1861) [1914]
Archcliffe (Martello)
Tnl Opened out 1897
1860 SE
Clo 1995

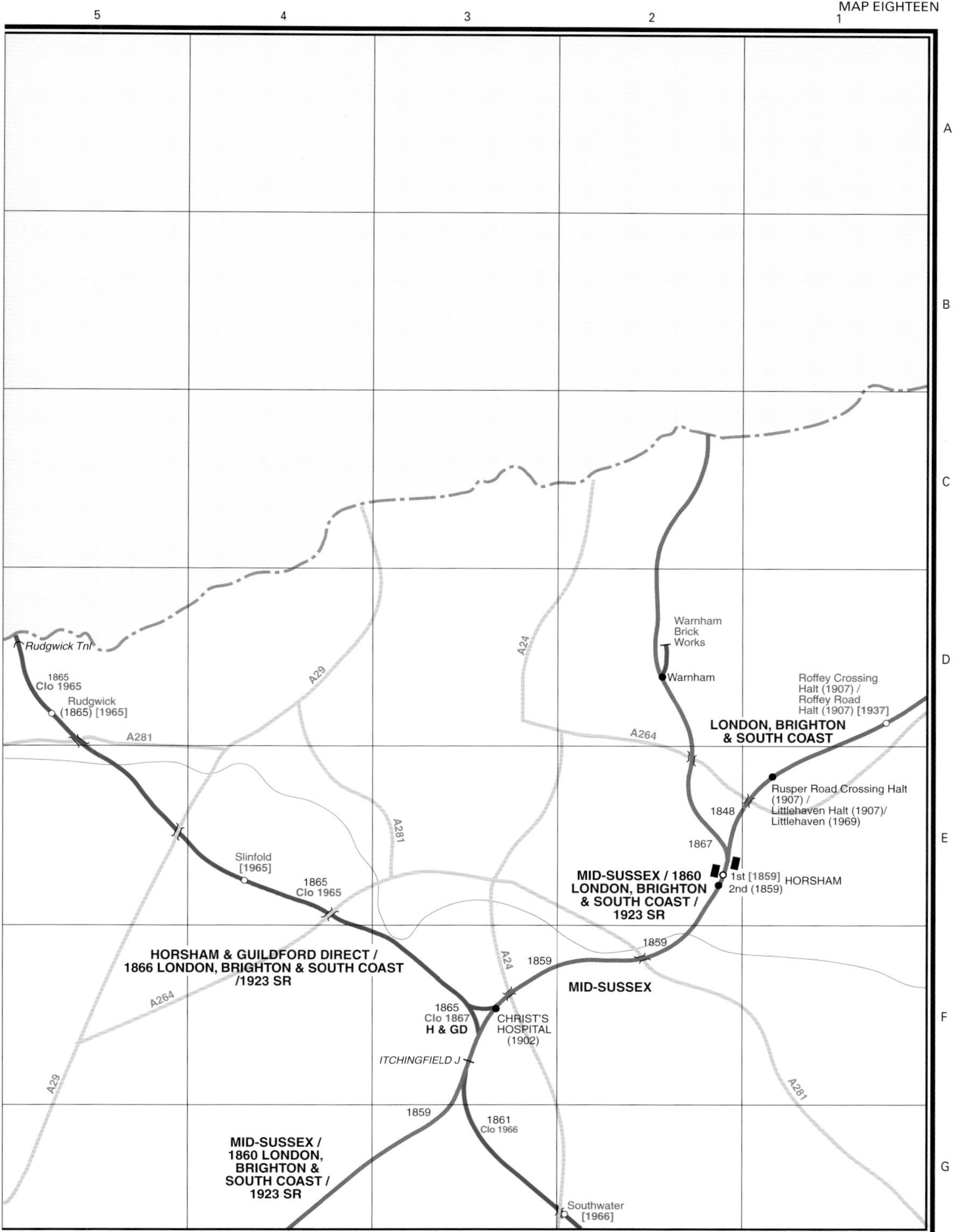

5
4
3
2
1
A
B
C
D
E
F
G
Rudgwick Tnl
1865
Clo 1965
Rudgwick
(1865) [1965]
A281
A29
A24
Warnham
Brick
Works
Warnham
Roffey Crossing
Halt (1907) /
Roffey Road
Halt (1907) [1937]
LONDON, BRIGHTON
& SOUTH COAST
A264
Rusper Road Crossing Halt
(1907) /
Littlehaven Halt (1907)/
Littlehaven (1969)
1848
1867
A281
Slinfold
[1965]
1865
Clo 1965
MID-SUSSEX / 1860
LONDON, BRIGHTON
& SOUTH COAST /
1923 SR
1st [1859]
2nd (1859)
HORSHAM
1859
HORSHAM & GUILDFORD DIRECT /
1866 LONDON, BRIGHTON & SOUTH COAST
/1923 SR
A24
1859
MID-SUSSEX
A264
1865
Clo 1867
H & GD
CHRIST'S
HOSPITAL
(1902)
ITCHINGFIELD J
A29
A281
1859
1861
Clo 1966
MID-SUSSEX /
1860 LONDON,
BRIGHTON &
SOUTH COAST /
1923 SR
Southwater
[1966]

MAP NINETEEN

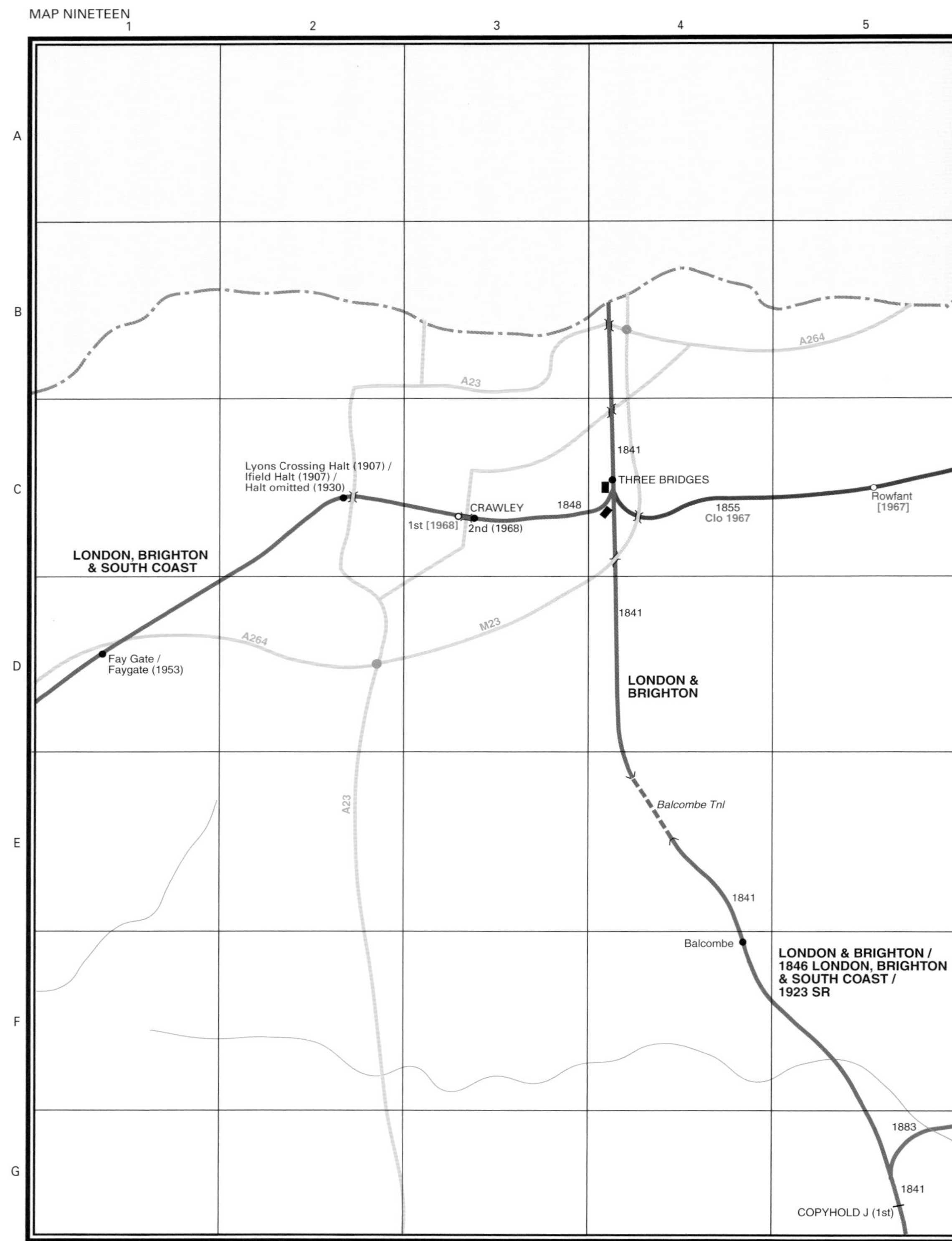

1
2
3
4
5
A
B
C
D
E
F
G
A23
A264
1841
Lyons Crossing Halt (1907) /
Ifield Halt (1907) /
Halt omitted (1930)
THREE BRIDGES
CRAWLEY
1848
1st [1968]
2nd (1968)
1855
Clo 1967
Rowfant
[1967]
LONDON, BRIGHTON
& SOUTH COAST
1841
M23
A264
Fay Gate /
Faygate (1953)
LONDON &
BRIGHTON
A23
Balcombe Tnl
1841
Balcombe
LONDON & BRIGHTON /
1846 LONDON, BRIGHTON
& SOUTH COAST /
1923 SR
1883
1841
COPYHOLD J (1st)

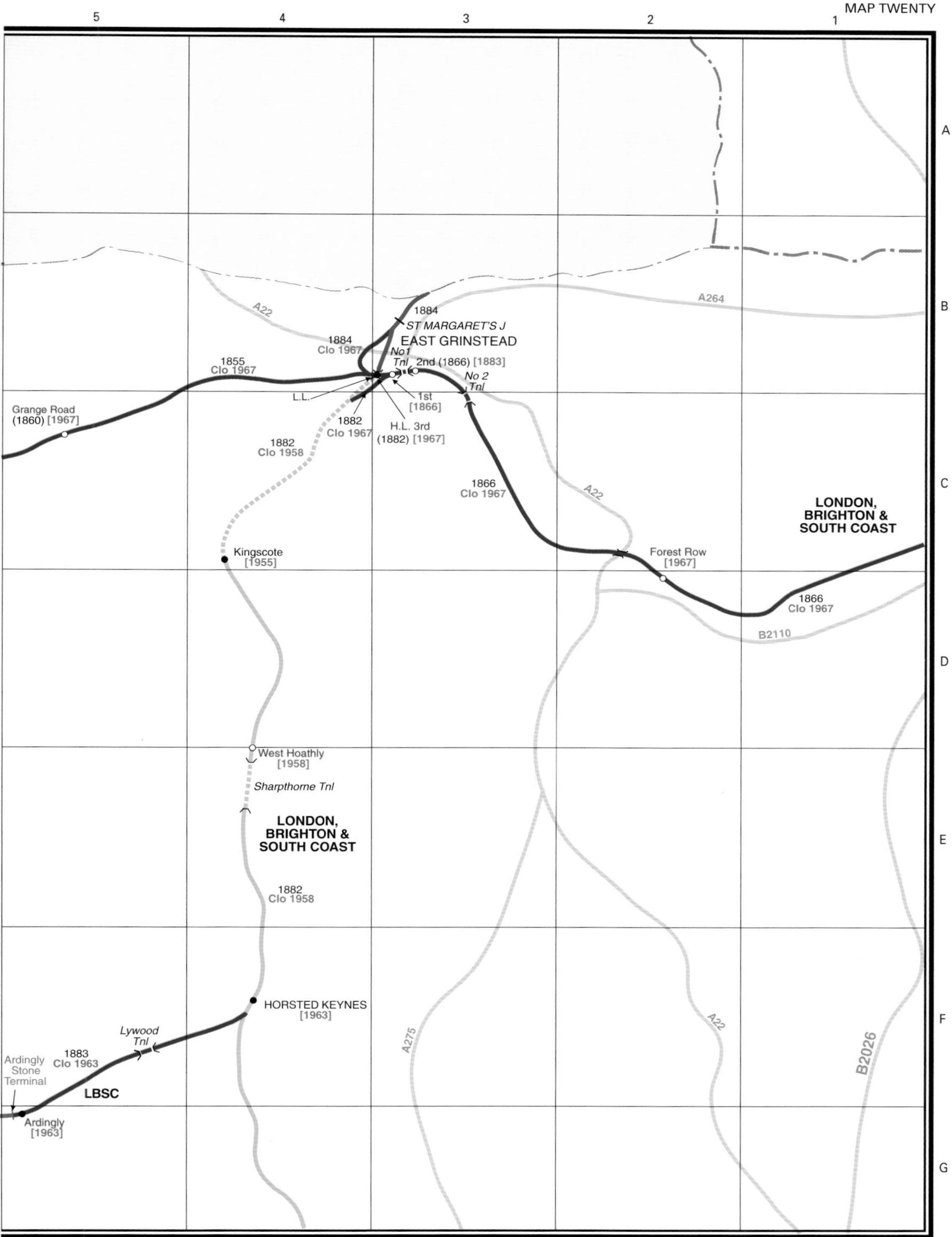
5
4
3
2
1
A
B
C
D
E
F
G
A22
A264
1884
ST MARGARET'S J
EAST GRINSTEAD
1884
Clo 1967
No1
Tnl
2nd (1866) [1883]
No 2
Tnl
1855
Clo 1967
L.L.
1st
[1866]
Grange Road
(1860) [1967]
1882
Clo 1967
H.L. 3rd
(1882) [1967]
1882
Clo 1958
1866
Clo 1967
A22
LONDON,
BRIGHTON &
SOUTH COAST
Kingscote
[1955]
Forest Row
[1967]
1866
Clo 1967
B2110
West Hoathly
[1958]
Sharpthorne Tnl
LONDON,
BRIGHTON &
SOUTH COAST
1882
Clo 1958
HORSTED KEYNES
[1963]
Lywood
Tnl
1883
Clo 1963
Ardingly
Stone
Terminal
LBSC
Ardingly
[1963]
A275
A22
B2026

MAP TWENTY ONE

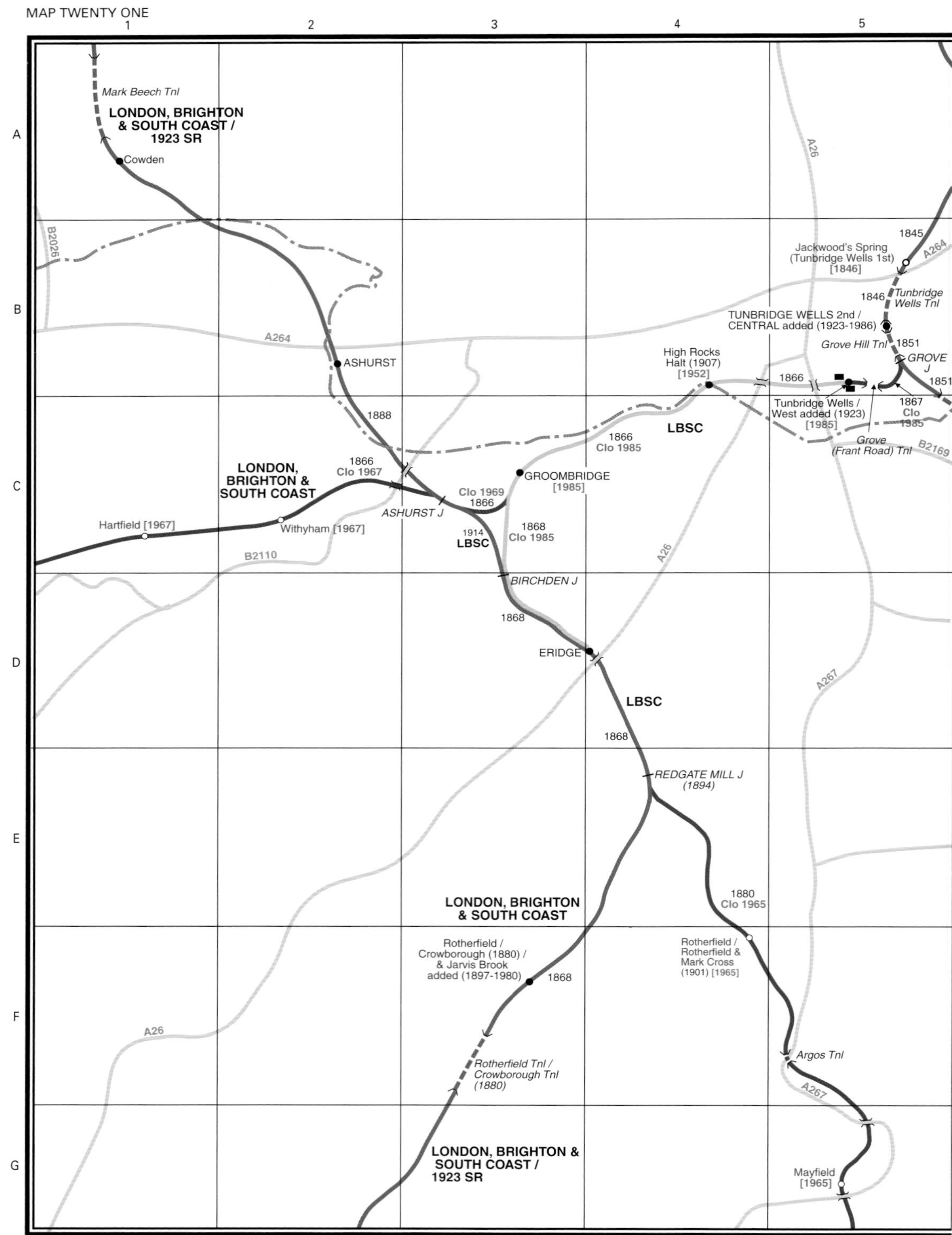

1
2
3
4
5
A
B
C
D
E
F
G
Mark Beech Tnl
LONDON, BRIGHTON & SOUTH COAST / 1923 SR
Cowden
B2026
A264
ASHURST
1888
A26
1845
Jackwood's Spring (Tunbridge Wells 1st) [1846]
A264
1846
Tunbridge Wells Tnl
TUNBRIDGE WELLS 2nd / CENTRAL added (1923-1986)
Grove Hill Tnl
1851
GROVE J
1851
High Rocks Halt (1907) [1952]
1866
Tunbridge Wells / West added (1923) [1985]
1867 Clo 1985
Grove (Frant Road) Tnl
B2169
LBSC
1866 Clo 1985
1866 Clo 1967
LONDON, BRIGHTON & SOUTH COAST
GROOMBRIDGE [1985]
Clo 1969 1866
ASHURST J
Hartfield [1967]
Withyham [1967]
1914 LBSC
1868 Clo 1985
B2110
A26
BIRCHDEN J
1868
ERIDGE
LBSC
A267
1868
REDGATE MILL J (1894)
1880 Clo 1965
LONDON, BRIGHTON & SOUTH COAST
Rotherfield / Crowborough (1880) / & Jarvis Brook added (1897-1980)
1868
Rotherfield / Rotherfield & Mark Cross (1901) [1965]
A26
Argos Tnl
Rotherfield Tnl / Crowborough Tnl (1880)
A267
LONDON, BRIGHTON & SOUTH COAST / 1923 SR
Mayfield [1965]

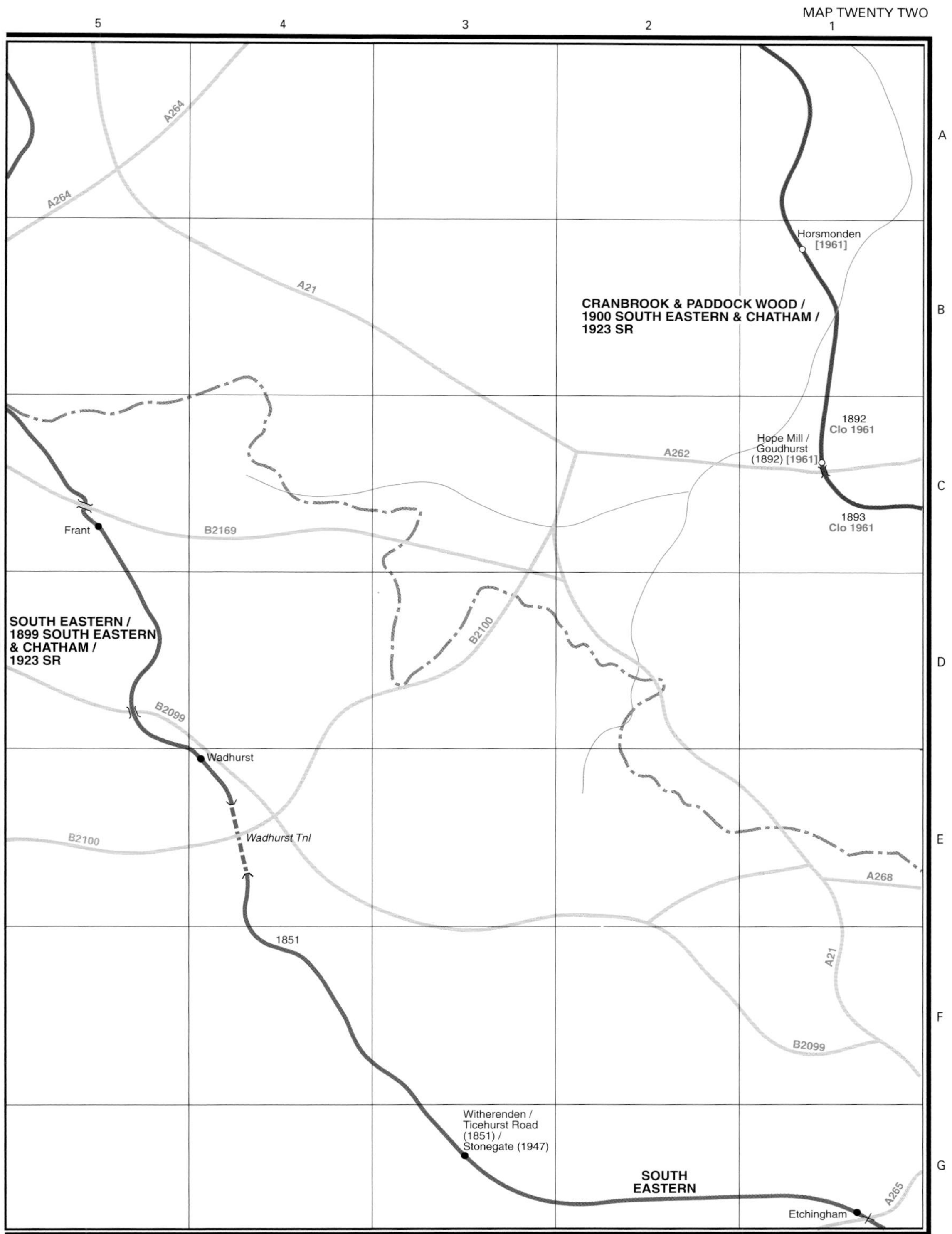
5
4
3
2
1
A
B
C
D
E
F
G
A264
A264
A21
Horsmonden
[1961]
CRANBROOK & PADDOCK WOOD /
1900 SOUTH EASTERN & CHATHAM /
1923 SR
1892
Clo 1961
Hope Mill /
Goudhurst
(1892) [1961]
A262
1893
Clo 1961
Frant
B2169
SOUTH EASTERN /
1899 SOUTH EASTERN
& CHATHAM /
1923 SR
B2100
B2099
Wadhurst
B2100
Wadhurst Tnl
A268
1851
A21
B2099
Witherenden /
Ticehurst Road
(1851) /
Stonegate (1947)
SOUTH
EASTERN
A265
Etchingham

MAP TWENTY THREE

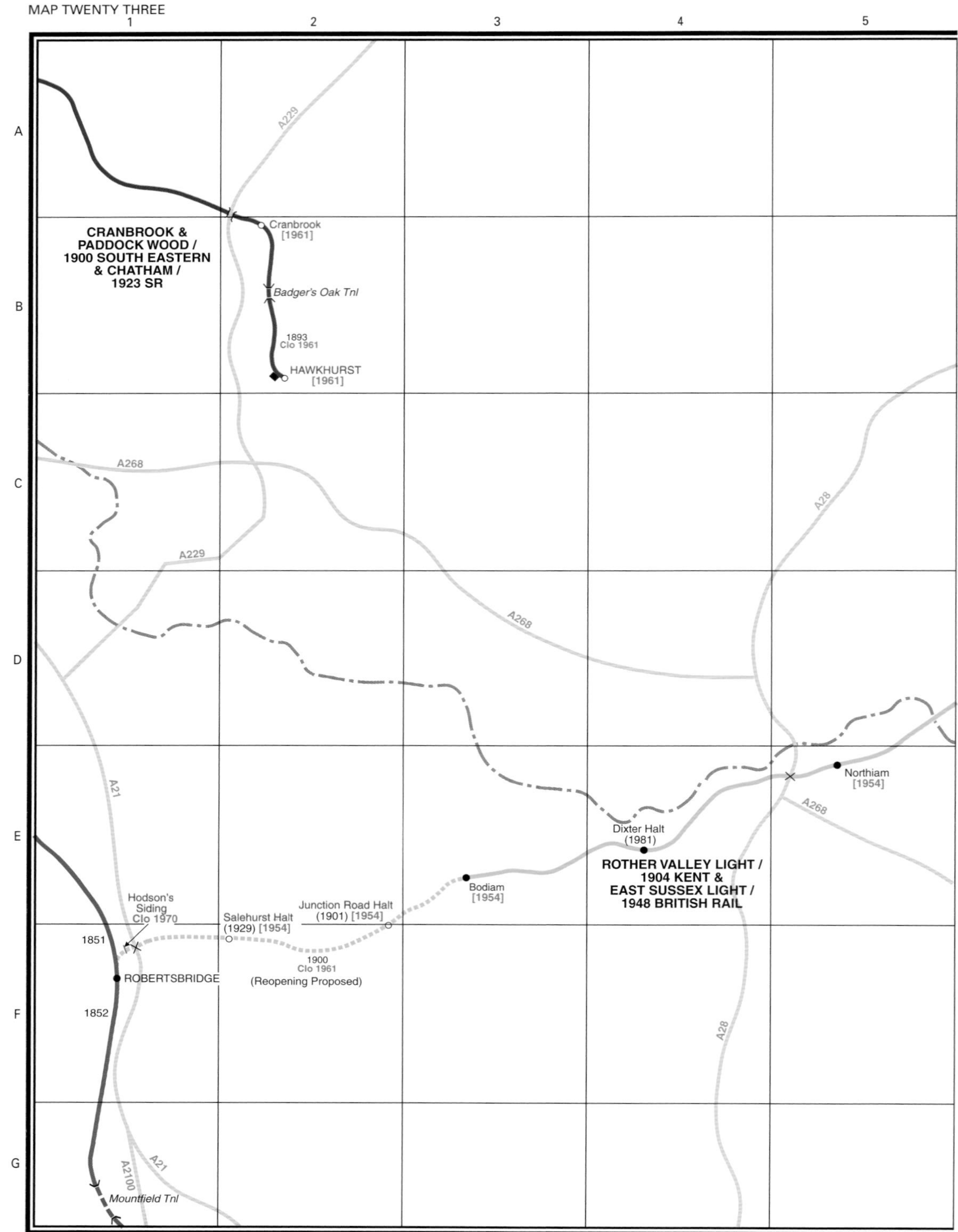

1
2
3
4
5
A
B
C
D
E
F
G
A229
CRANBROOK & PADDOCK WOOD / 1900 SOUTH EASTERN & CHATHAM / 1923 SR
Cranbrook [1961]
Badger's Oak Tnl
1893 Clo 1961
HAWKHURST [1961]
A268
A229
A28
A268
A21
Northiam [1954]
A268
Dixter Halt (1981)
ROTHER VALLEY LIGHT / 1904 KENT & EAST SUSSEX LIGHT / 1948 BRITISH RAIL
Bodiam [1954]
Hodson's Siding Clo 1970
Salehurst Halt (1929) [1954]
Junction Road Halt (1901) [1954]
1851
ROBERTSBRIDGE
1900 Clo 1961
(Reopening Proposed)
1852
A28
A2100
A21
Mountfield Tnl

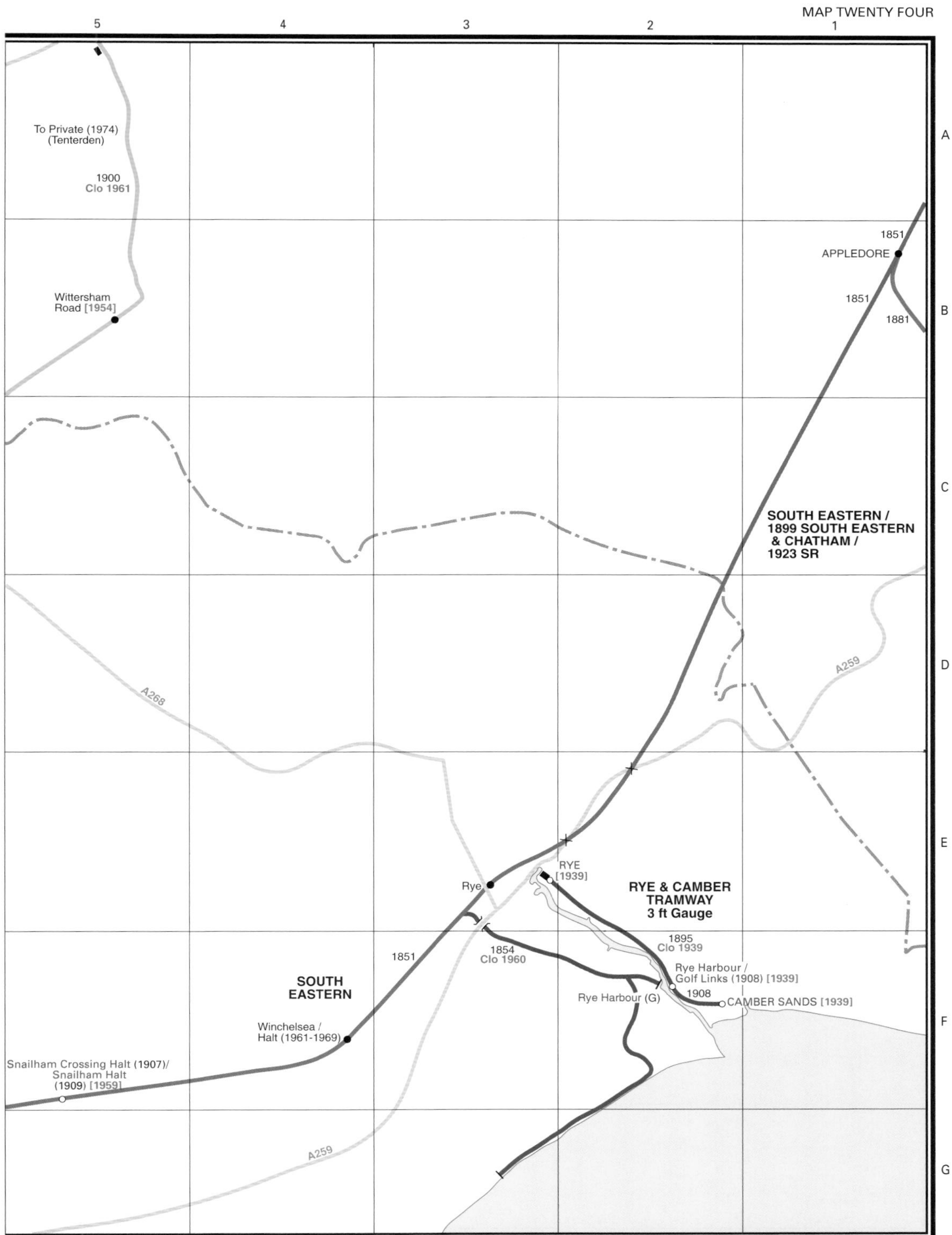
5
4
3
2
1
A
B
C
D
E
F
G
To Private (1974)
(Tenterden)
1900
Clo 1961
Wittersham
Road [1954]
1851
APPLEDORE
1851
1881
SOUTH EASTERN /
1899 SOUTH EASTERN
& CHATHAM /
1923 SR
A268
A259
RYE
[1939]
Rye
RYE & CAMBER
TRAMWAY
3 ft Gauge
1895
Clo 1939
1854
Clo 1960
1851
Rye Harbour /
Golf Links (1908) [1939]
1908
Rye Harbour (G)
CAMBER SANDS [1939]
SOUTH
EASTERN
Winchelsea /
Halt (1961-1969)
Snailham Crossing Halt (1907)/
Snailham Halt
(1909) [1959]
A259

MAP TWENTY FIVE

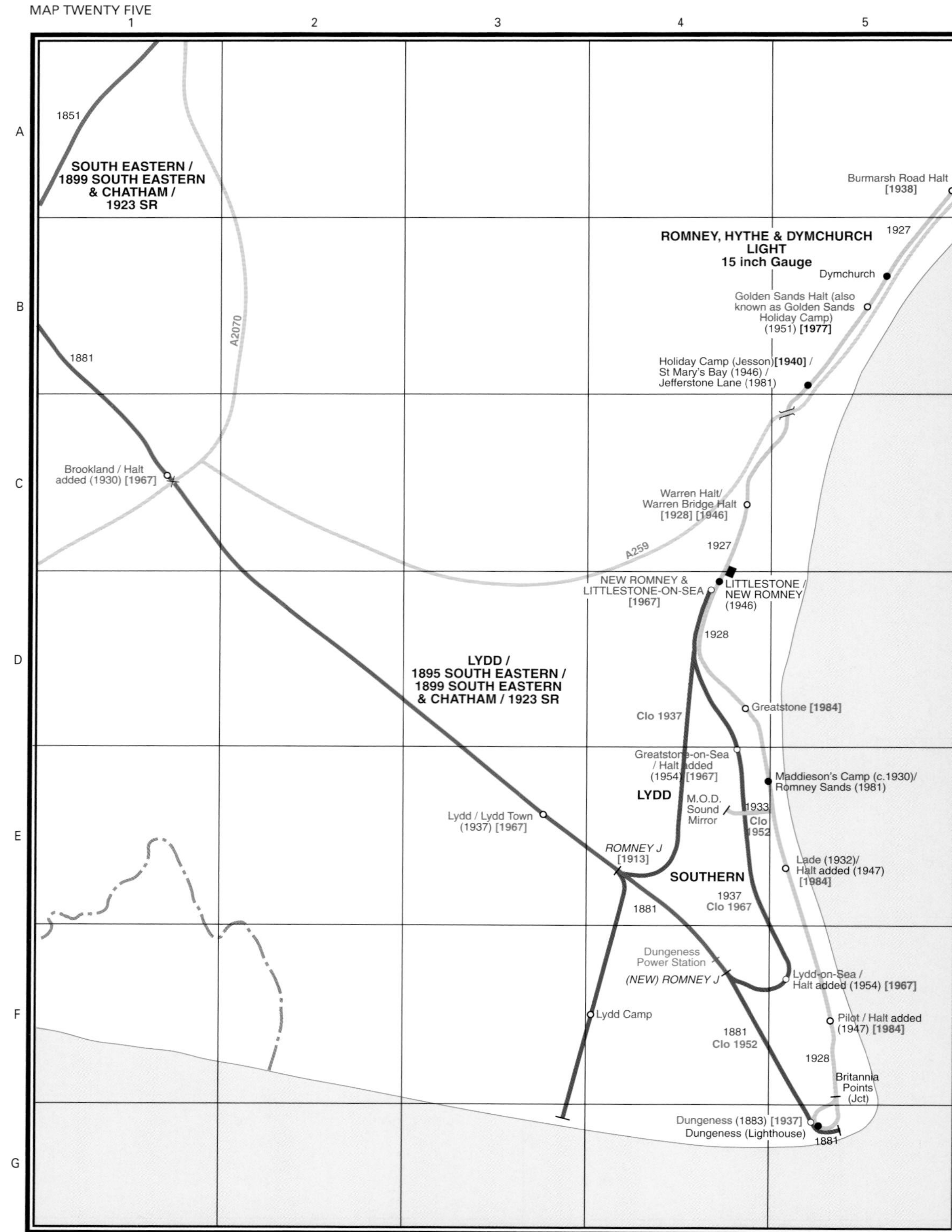
1
2
3
4
5
A
B
C
D
E
F
G
1851
SOUTH EASTERN /
1899 SOUTH EASTERN
& CHATHAM /
1923 SR
A2070
1881
Brookland / Halt
added (1930) [1967]
Burmarsh Road Halt
[1938]
1927
ROMNEY, HYTHE & DYMCHURCH
LIGHT
15 inch Gauge
Dymchurch
Golden Sands Halt (also
known as Golden Sands
Holiday Camp)
(1951) [1977]
Holiday Camp (Jesson)[1940] /
St Mary's Bay (1946) /
Jefferstone Lane (1981)
Warren Halt/
Warren Bridge Halt
[1928] [1946]
A259
1927
NEW ROMNEY &
LITTLESTONE-ON-SEA
[1967]
LITTLESTONE /
NEW ROMNEY
(1946)
1928
LYDD /
1895 SOUTH EASTERN /
1899 SOUTH EASTERN
& CHATHAM / 1923 SR
Greatstone [1984]
Clo 1937
Greatstone-on-Sea
/ Halt added
(1954) [1967]
Maddieson's Camp (c.1930)/
Romney Sands (1981)
LYDD
M.O.D.
Sound
Mirror
1933
Clo
1952
Lydd / Lydd Town
(1937) [1967]
ROMNEY J
[1913]
Lade (1932)/
Halt added (1947)
[1984]
SOUTHERN
1937
Clo 1967
1881
Dungeness
Power Station
(NEW) ROMNEY J
Lydd-on-Sea /
Halt added (1954) [1967]
Lydd Camp
Pilot / Halt added
(1947) [1984]
1881
Clo 1952
1928
Britannia
Points
(Jct)
Dungeness (1883) [1937]
Dungeness (Lighthouse)
1881

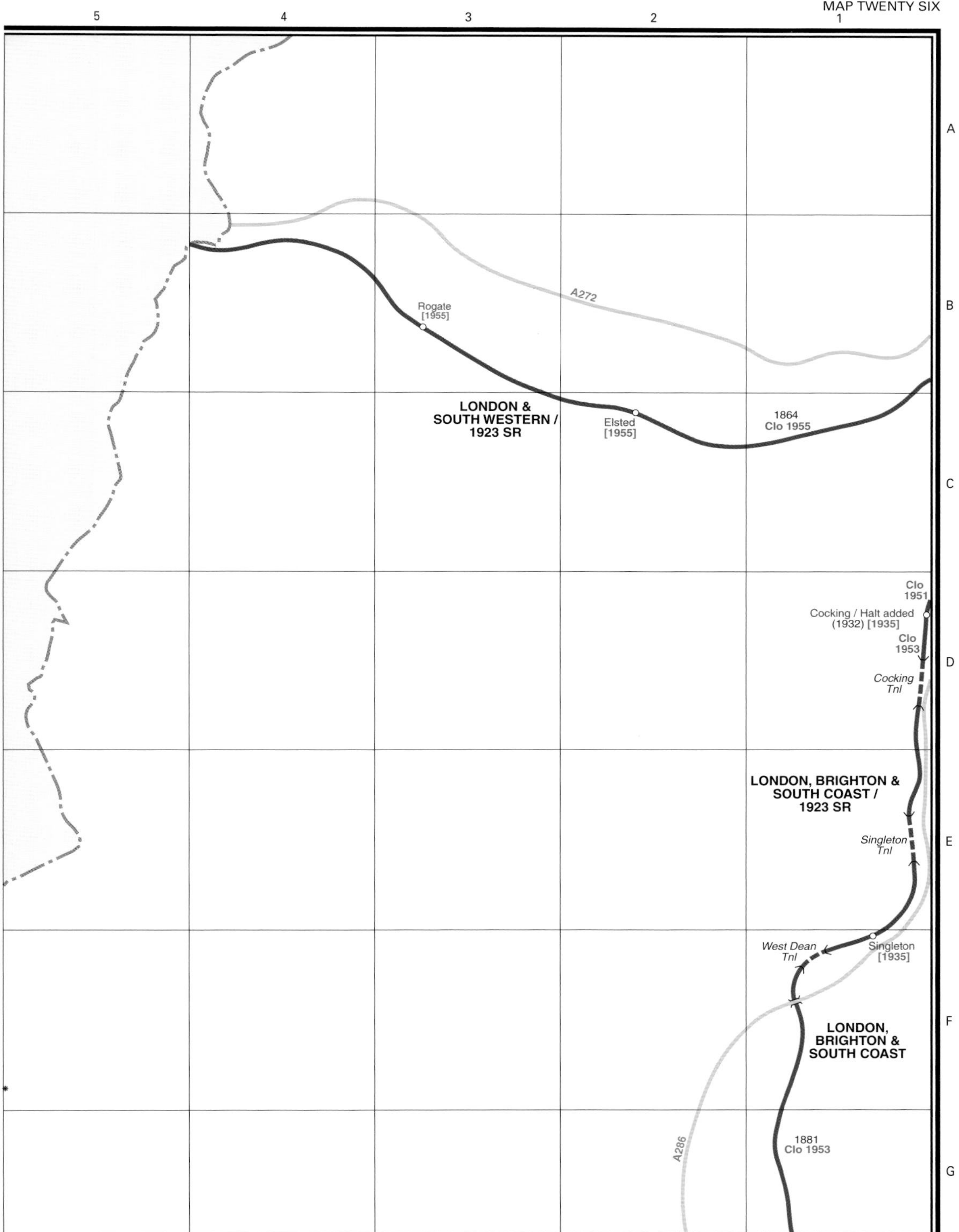
5
4
3
2
1
A
B
C
D
E
F
G
A272
Rogate
[1955]
LONDON &
SOUTH WESTERN /
1923 SR
Elsted
[1955]
1864
Clo 1955
Clo
1951
Cocking / Halt added
(1932) [1935]
Clo
1953
Cocking
Tnl
LONDON, BRIGHTON &
SOUTH COAST /
1923 SR
Singleton
Tnl
West Dean
Tnl
Singleton
[1935]
LONDON,
BRIGHTON &
SOUTH COAST
A286
1881
Clo 1953

MAP TWENTY SEVEN

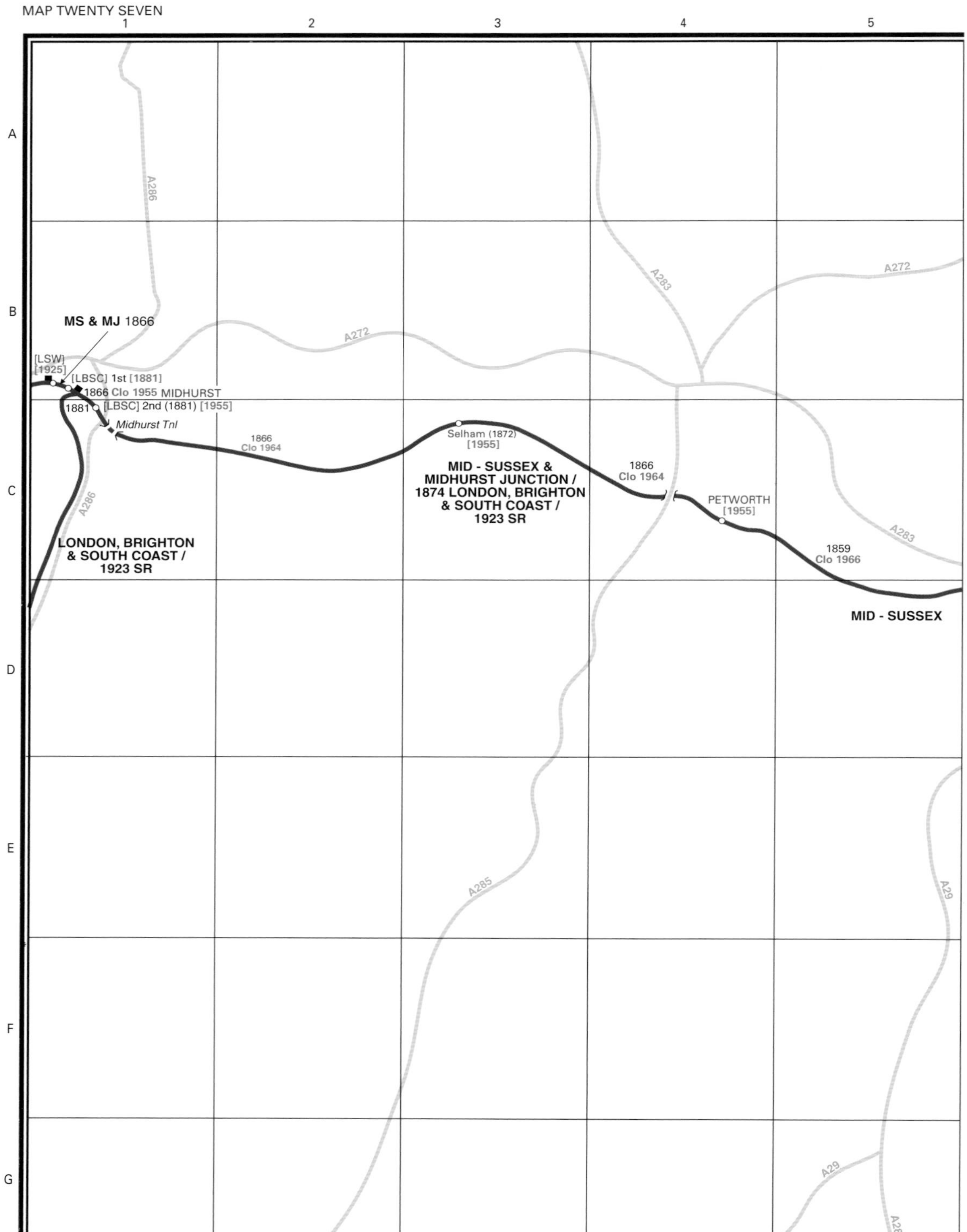

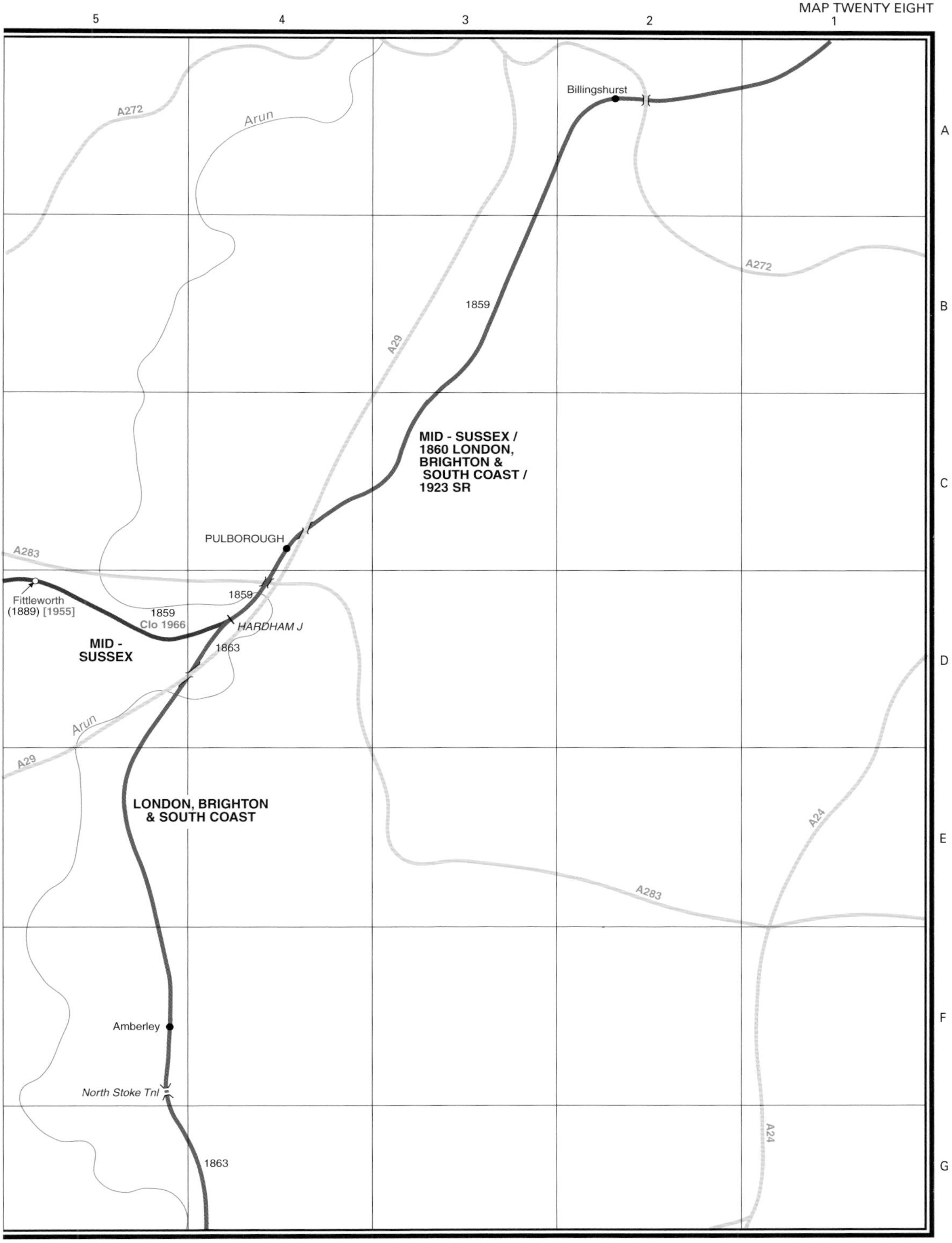

MAP TWENTY EIGHT

5 4 3 2 1

A B C D E F G

Billingshurst

A272

Arun

1859

A29

MID - SUSSEX /
1860 LONDON,
BRIGHTON &
SOUTH COAST /
1923 SR

PULBOROUGH

A283

Fittleworth
(1889) [1955]

1859
Clo 1966

1859

HARDHAM J

1863

MID -
SUSSEX

Arun

A29

LONDON, BRIGHTON
& SOUTH COAST

A24

A283

Amberley

North Stoke Tnl

1863

A24

MAP TWENTY NINE

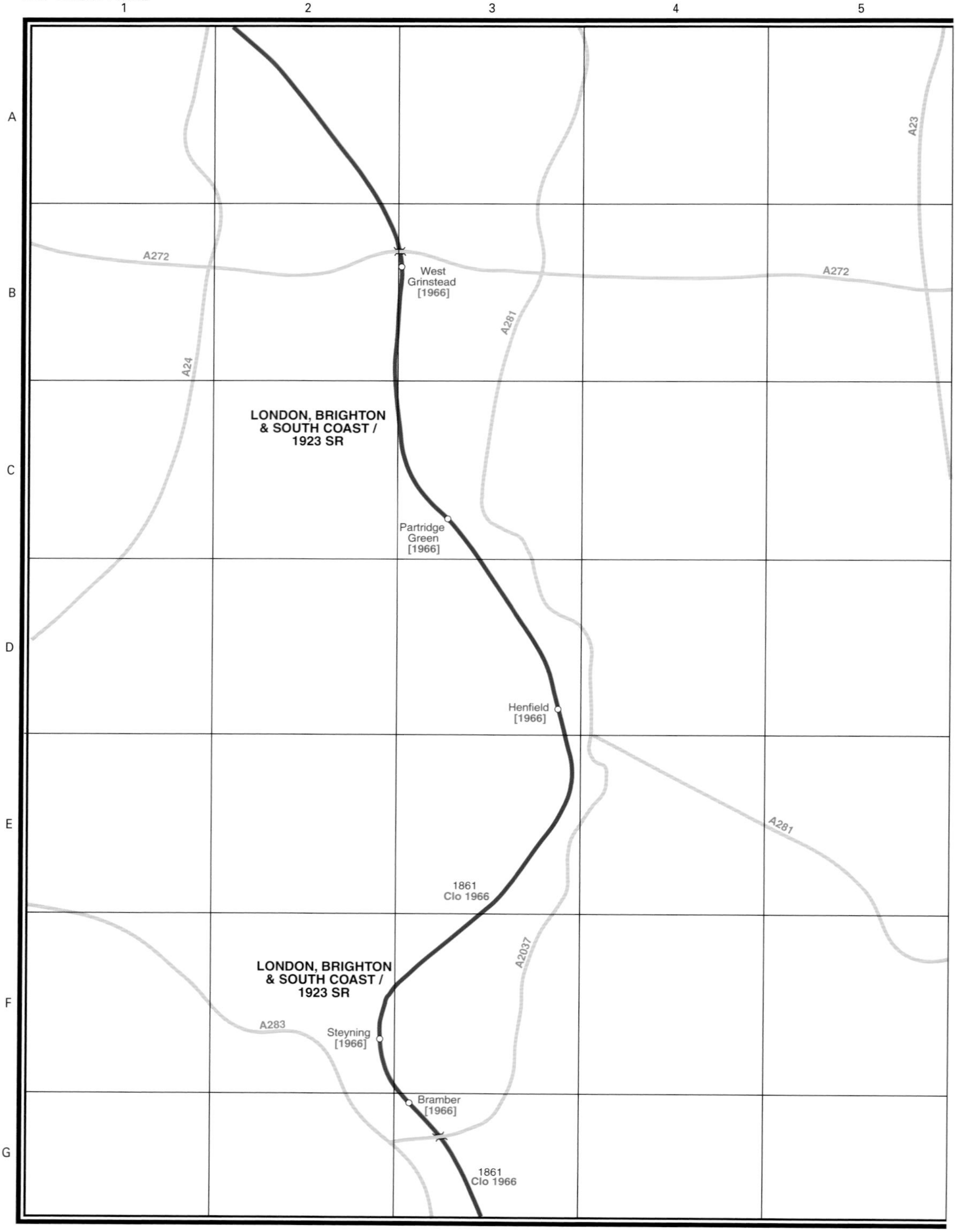

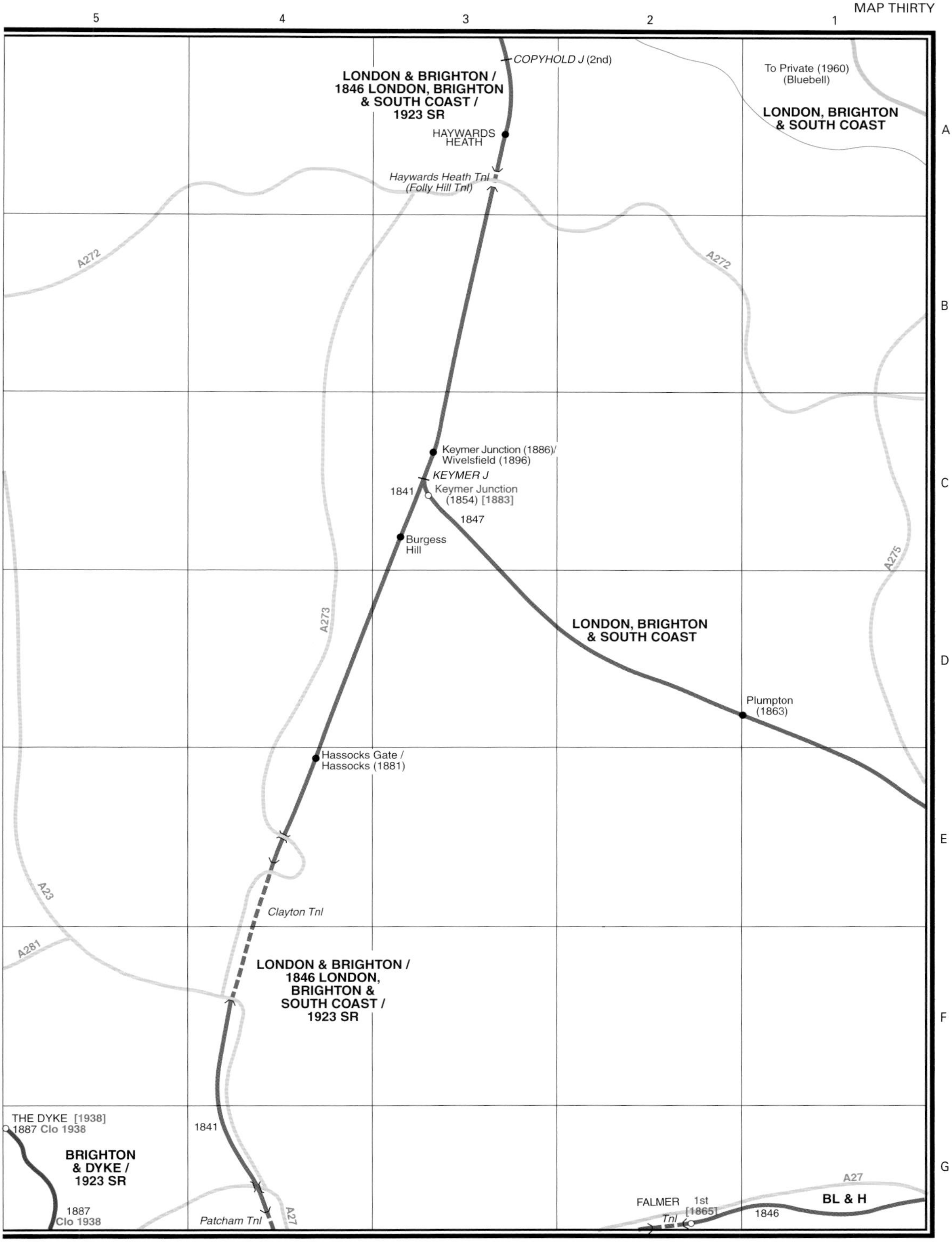

5 4 3 2 1

A B C D E F G

COPYHOLD J (2nd)

LONDON & BRIGHTON / 1846 LONDON, BRIGHTON & SOUTH COAST / 1923 SR

HAYWARDS HEATH

Haywards Heath Tnl (Folly Hill Tnl)

To Private (1960) (Bluebell)

LONDON, BRIGHTON & SOUTH COAST

A272

A272

Keymer Junction (1886)/ Wivelsfield (1896)

KEYMER J

1841

Keymer Junction (1854) [1883]

1847

Burgess Hill

A275

A273

LONDON, BRIGHTON & SOUTH COAST

Plumpton (1863)

Hassocks Gate / Hassocks (1881)

A23

Clayton Tnl

A281

LONDON & BRIGHTON / 1846 LONDON, BRIGHTON & SOUTH COAST / 1923 SR

THE DYKE [1938]
1887 Clo 1938

1841

BRIGHTON & DYKE / 1923 SR

1887
Clo 1938

Patcham Tnl

A27

A27

FALMER 1st [1865]

Tnl

1846

BL & H

MAP THIRTY ONE

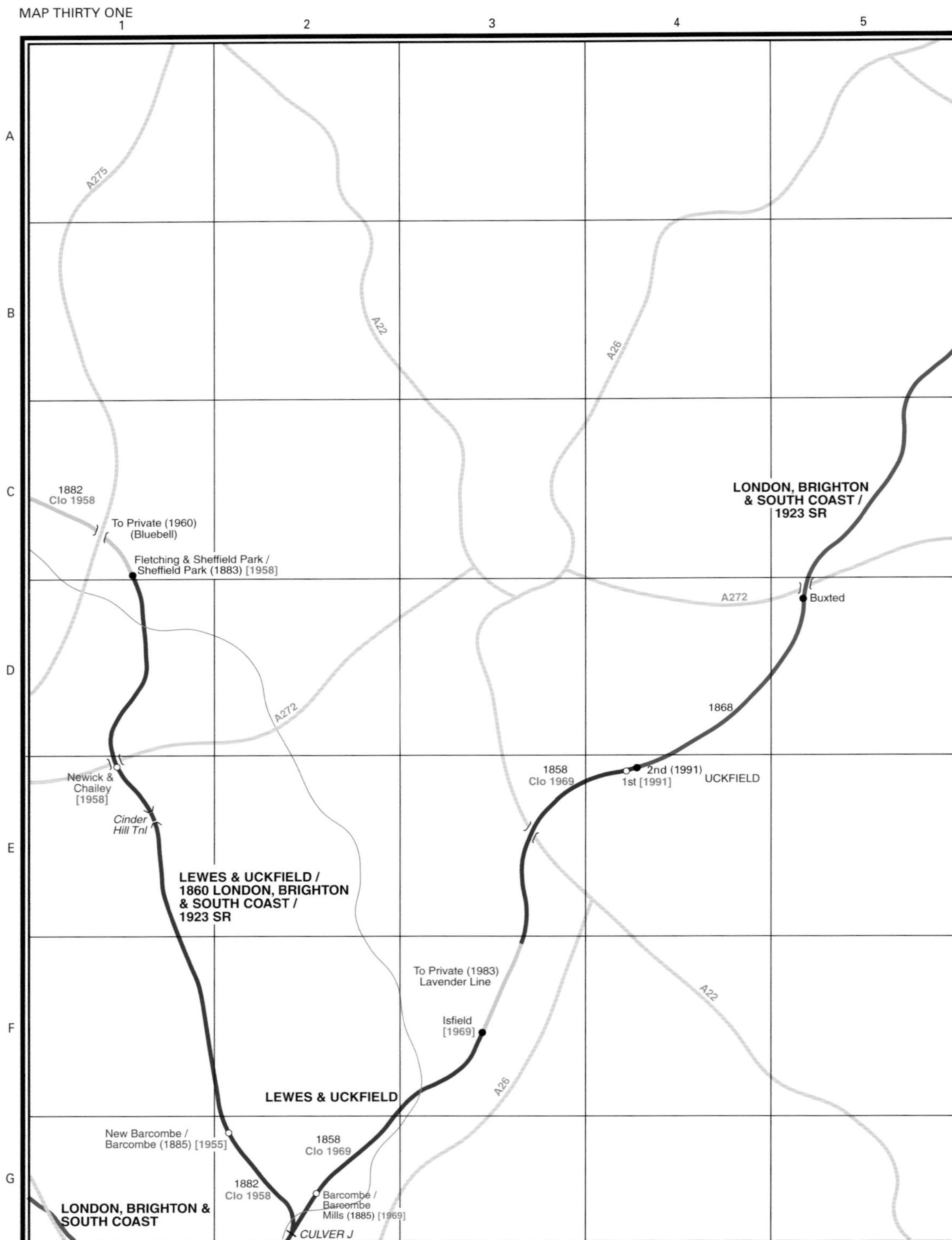
1
2
3
4
5
A
B
C
D
E
F
G
A275
A22
A26
A272
1882
Clo 1958
To Private (1960)
(Bluebell)
Fletching & Sheffield Park /
Sheffield Park (1883) [1958]
LONDON, BRIGHTON
& SOUTH COAST /
1923 SR
Buxted
1868
Newick &
Chailey
[1958]
Cinder
Hill Tnl
1858
Clo 1969
2nd (1991)
1st [1991]
UCKFIELD
LEWES & UCKFIELD /
1860 LONDON, BRIGHTON
& SOUTH COAST /
1923 SR
To Private (1983)
Lavender Line
Isfield
[1969]
LEWES & UCKFIELD
New Barcombe /
Barcombe (1885) [1955]
1858
Clo 1969
1882
Clo 1958
Barcombe /
Barcombe
Mills (1885) [1969]
LONDON, BRIGHTON &
SOUTH COAST
CULVER J

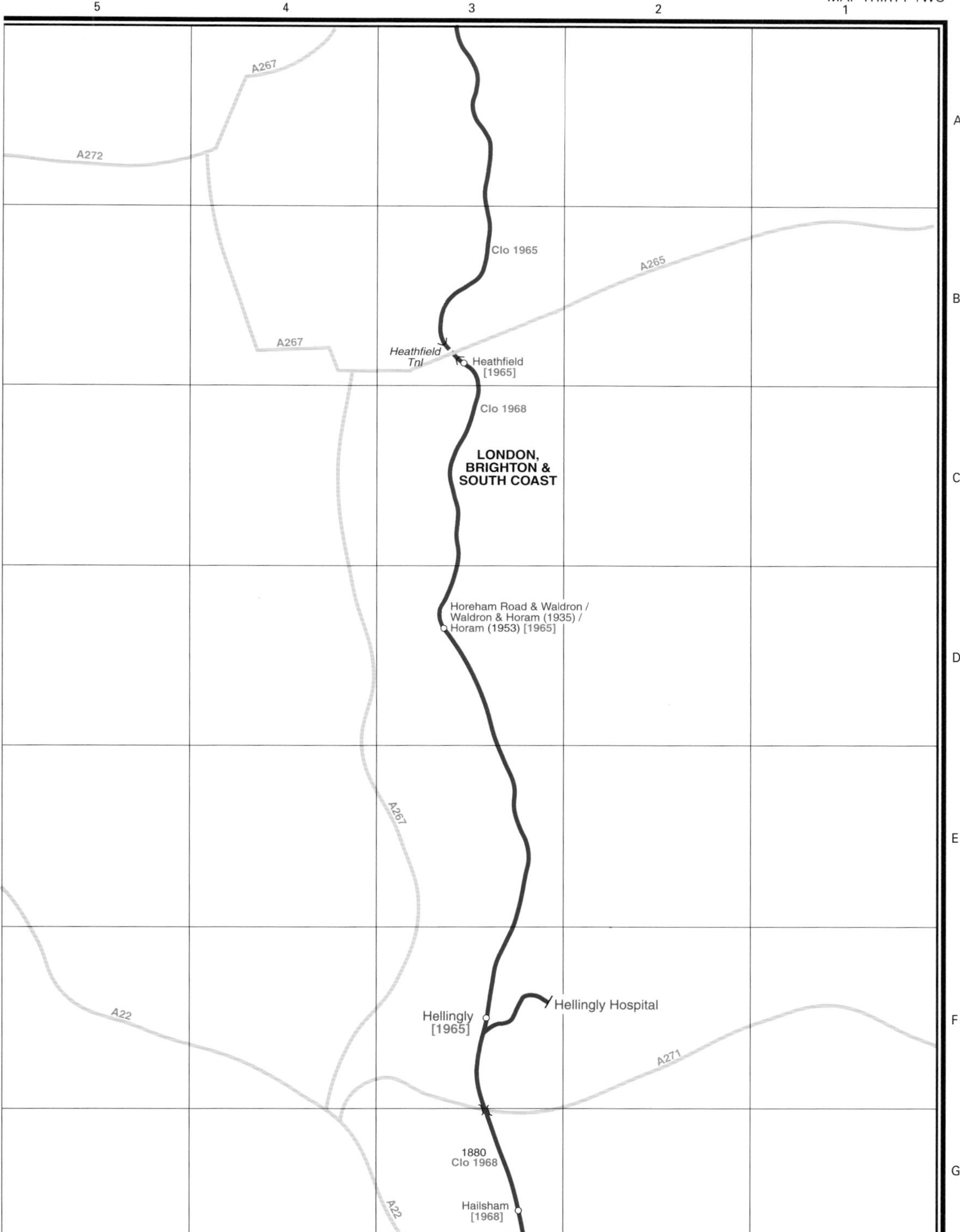
5
4
3
2
1
A
B
C
D
E
F
G
A267
A272
Clo 1965
A265
A267
Heathfield Tnl
Heathfield [1965]
Clo 1968
LONDON, BRIGHTON & SOUTH COAST
Horeham Road & Waldron / Waldron & Horam (1935) / Horam (1953) [1965]
A267
Hellingly Hospital
Hellingly [1965]
A22
A271
1880 Clo 1968
Hailsham [1968]
A22

MAP THIRTY THREE

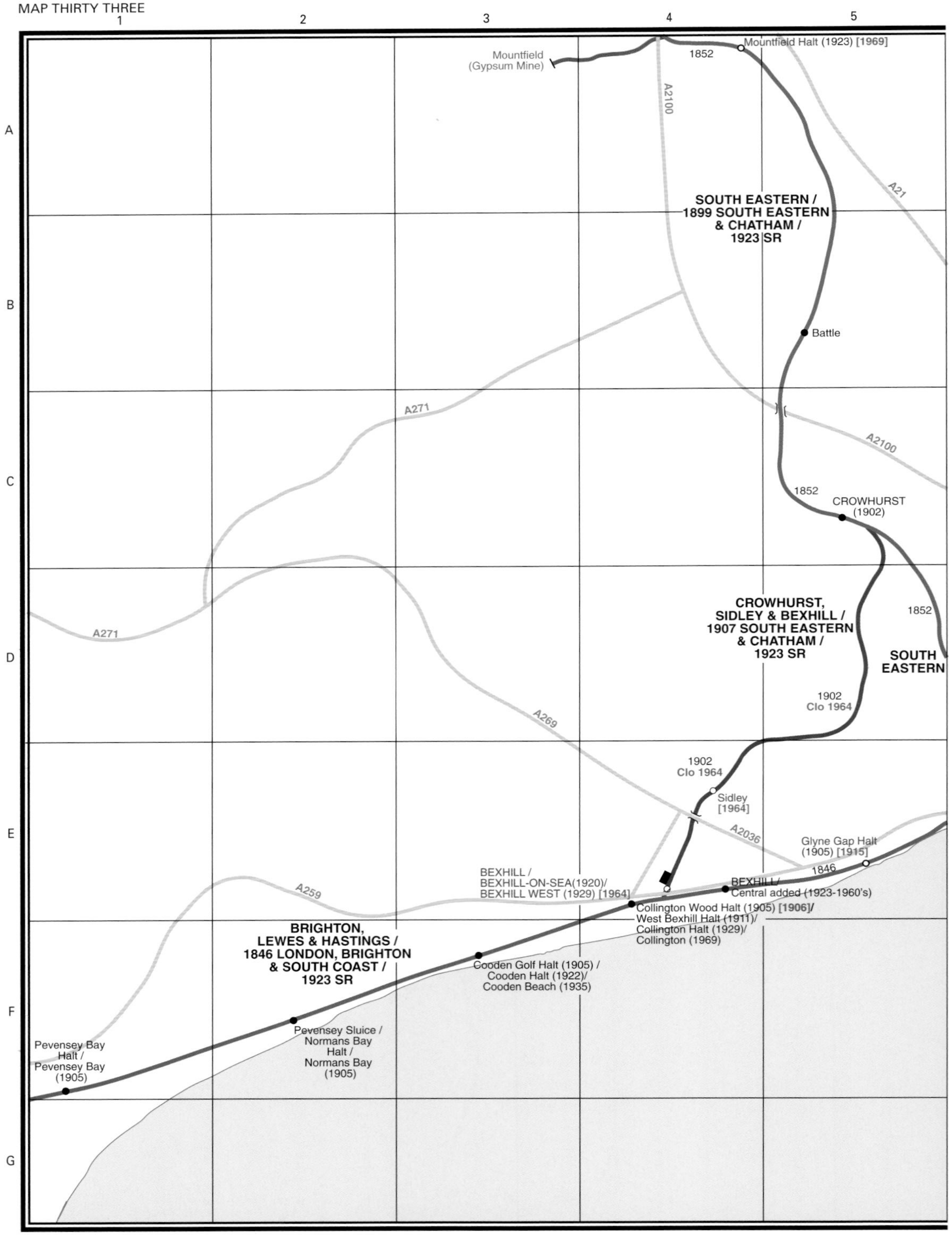

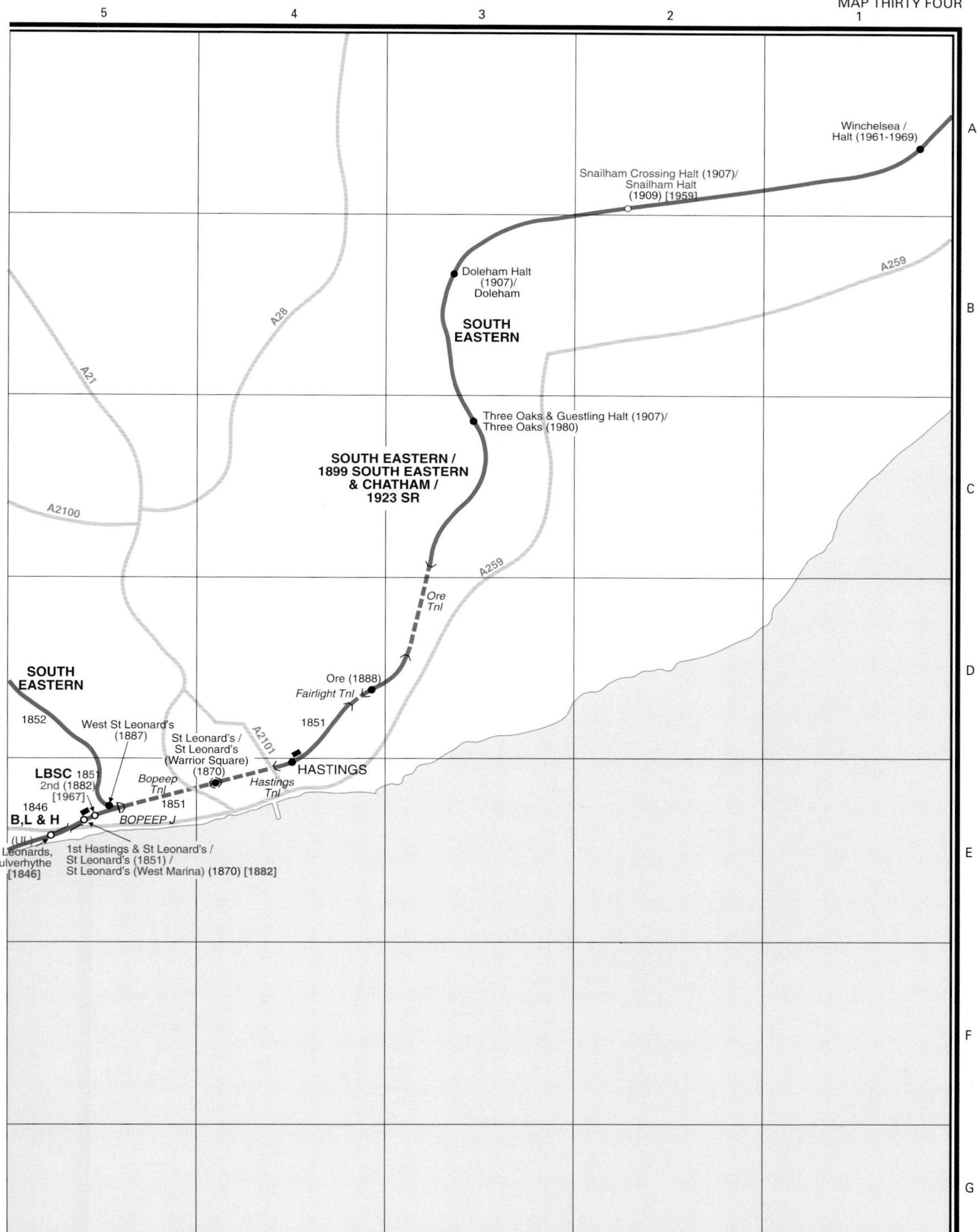
5
4
3
2
1
A
B
C
D
E
F
G
Winchelsea /
Halt (1961-1969)
Snailham Crossing Halt (1907)/
Snailham Halt
(1909) [1959]
Doleham Halt
(1907)/
Doleham
A259
A28
SOUTH
EASTERN
A21
Three Oaks & Guestling Halt (1907)/
Three Oaks (1980)
SOUTH EASTERN /
1899 SOUTH EASTERN
& CHATHAM /
1923 SR
A2100
A259
Ore
Tnl
SOUTH
EASTERN
Ore (1888)
Fairlight Tnl
1852
West St Leonard's
(1887)
1851
St Leonard's /
St Leonard's
(Warrior Square)
(1870)
A2101
HASTINGS
LBSC 1851
2nd (1882)
[1967]
Bopeep
Tnl
Hastings
Tnl
1851
1846
B,L & H
BOPEEP J
(UL)
St Leonards,
Bulverhythe
[1846]
1st Hastings & St Leonard's /
St Leonard's (1851) /
St Leonard's (West Marina) (1870) [1882]

MAP THIRTY FIVE

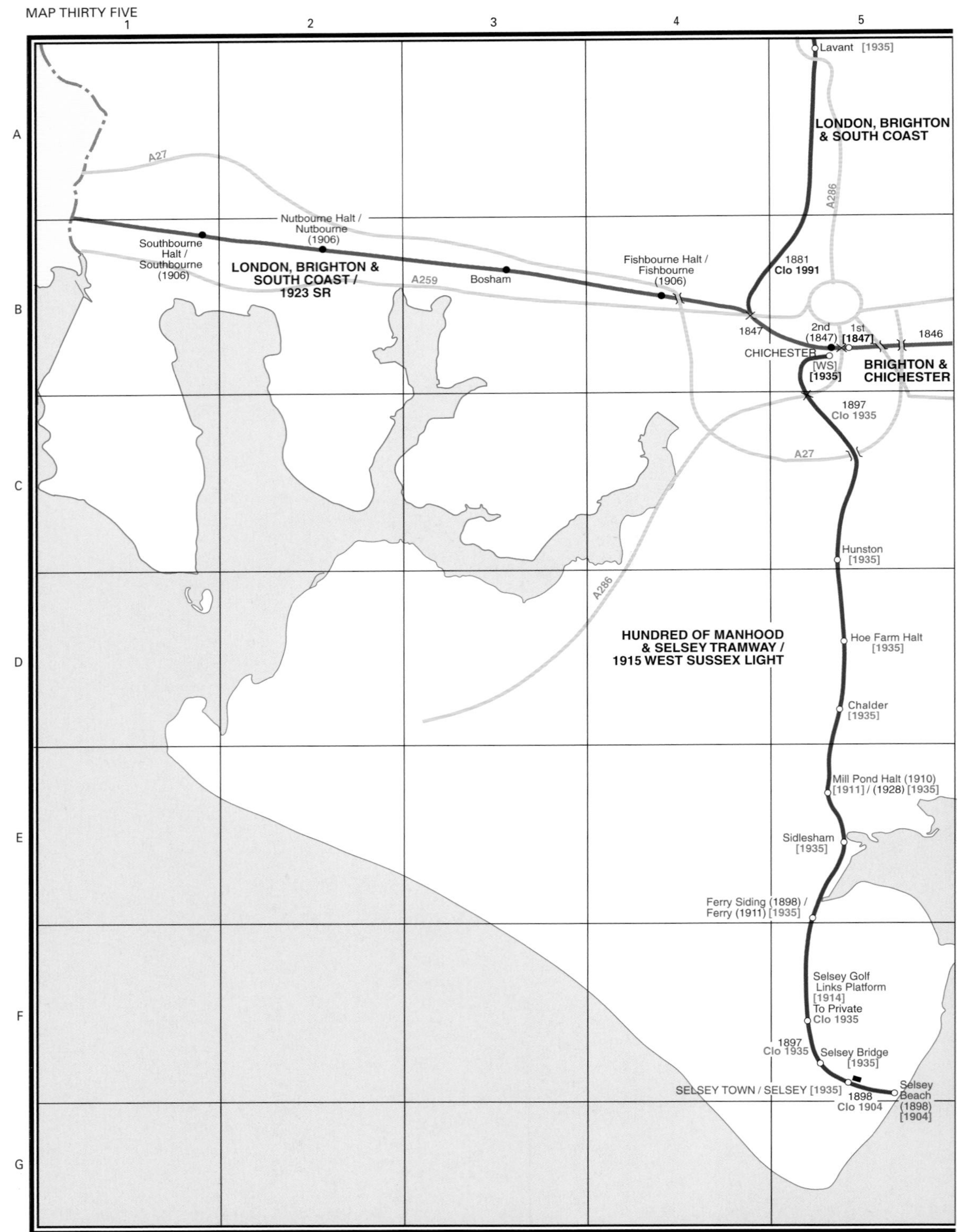
1
2
3
4
5
A
B
C
D
E
F
G
Lavant [1935]
LONDON, BRIGHTON & SOUTH COAST
A27
A286
Nutbourne Halt / Nutbourne (1906)
Southbourne Halt / Southbourne (1906)
LONDON, BRIGHTON & SOUTH COAST / 1923 SR
Bosham
A259
Fishbourne Halt / Fishbourne (1906)
1881
Clo 1991
1847
2nd (1847)
1st [1847]
1846
CHICHESTER
[WS] [1935]
BRIGHTON & CHICHESTER
1897
Clo 1935
A27
Hunston [1935]
A286
HUNDRED OF MANHOOD & SELSEY TRAMWAY / 1915 WEST SUSSEX LIGHT
Hoe Farm Halt [1935]
Chalder [1935]
Mill Pond Halt (1910) [1911] / (1928) [1935]
Sidlesham [1935]
Ferry Siding (1898) / Ferry (1911) [1935]
Selsey Golf Links Platform [1914] To Private Clo 1935
1897
Clo 1935
Selsey Bridge [1935]
SELSEY TOWN / SELSEY [1935]
1898
Clo 1904
Selsey Beach (1898) [1904]

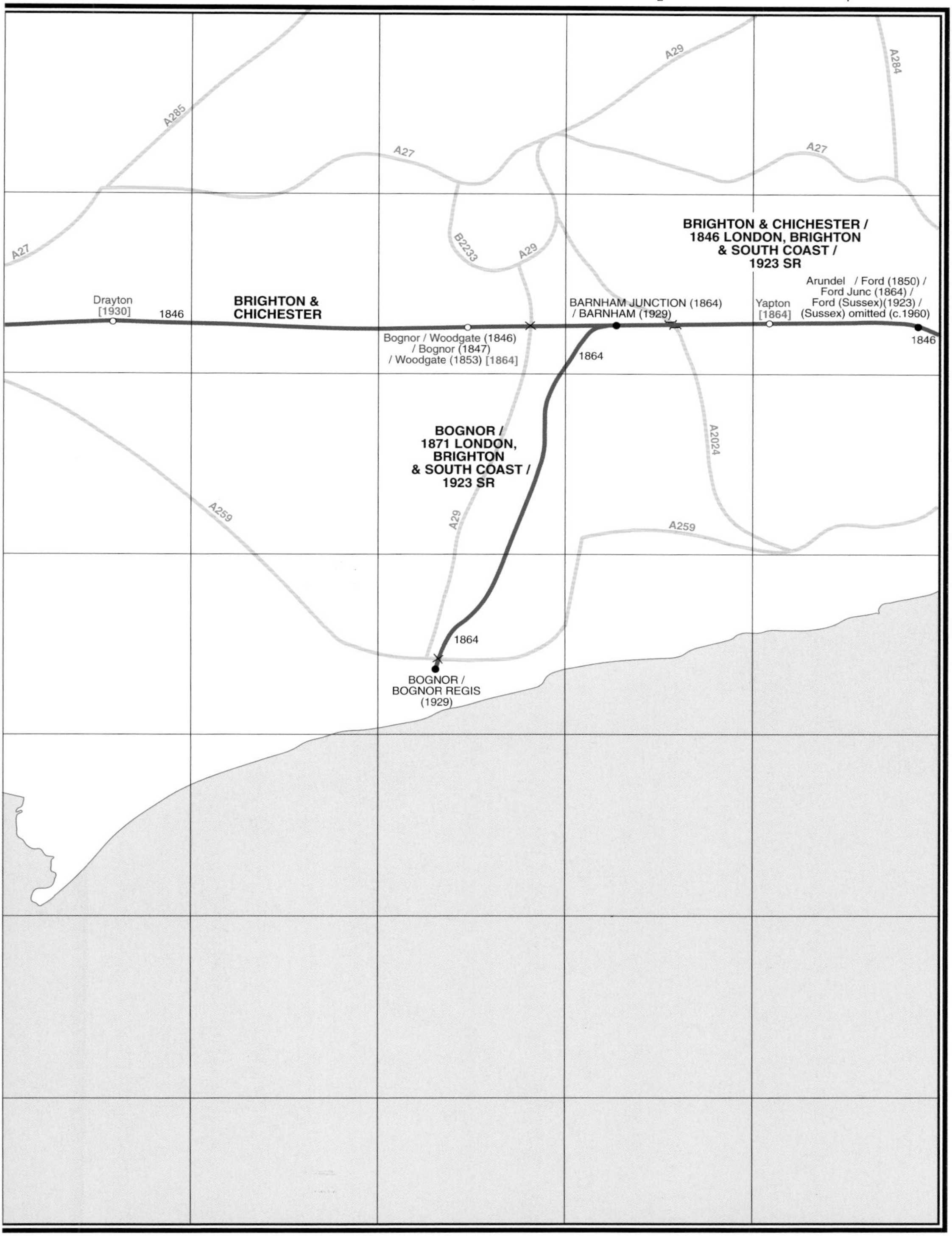

5
4
3
2
1
A
B
C
D
E
F
G
A285
A29
A284
A27
A27
A27
B2233
A29
BRIGHTON & CHICHESTER /
1846 LONDON, BRIGHTON
& SOUTH COAST /
1923 SR
Drayton
[1930]
1846
BRIGHTON &
CHICHESTER
BARNHAM JUNCTION (1864)
/ BARNHAM (1929)
Yapton
[1864]
Arundel / Ford (1850) /
Ford Junc (1864) /
Ford (Sussex)(1923) /
(Sussex) omitted (c.1960)
1846
Bognor / Woodgate (1846)
/ Bognor (1847)
/ Woodgate (1853) [1864]
1864
BOGNOR /
1871 LONDON,
BRIGHTON
& SOUTH COAST /
1923 SR
A2024
A259
A29
A259
1864
BOGNOR /
BOGNOR REGIS
(1929)

MAP THIRTY SEVEN

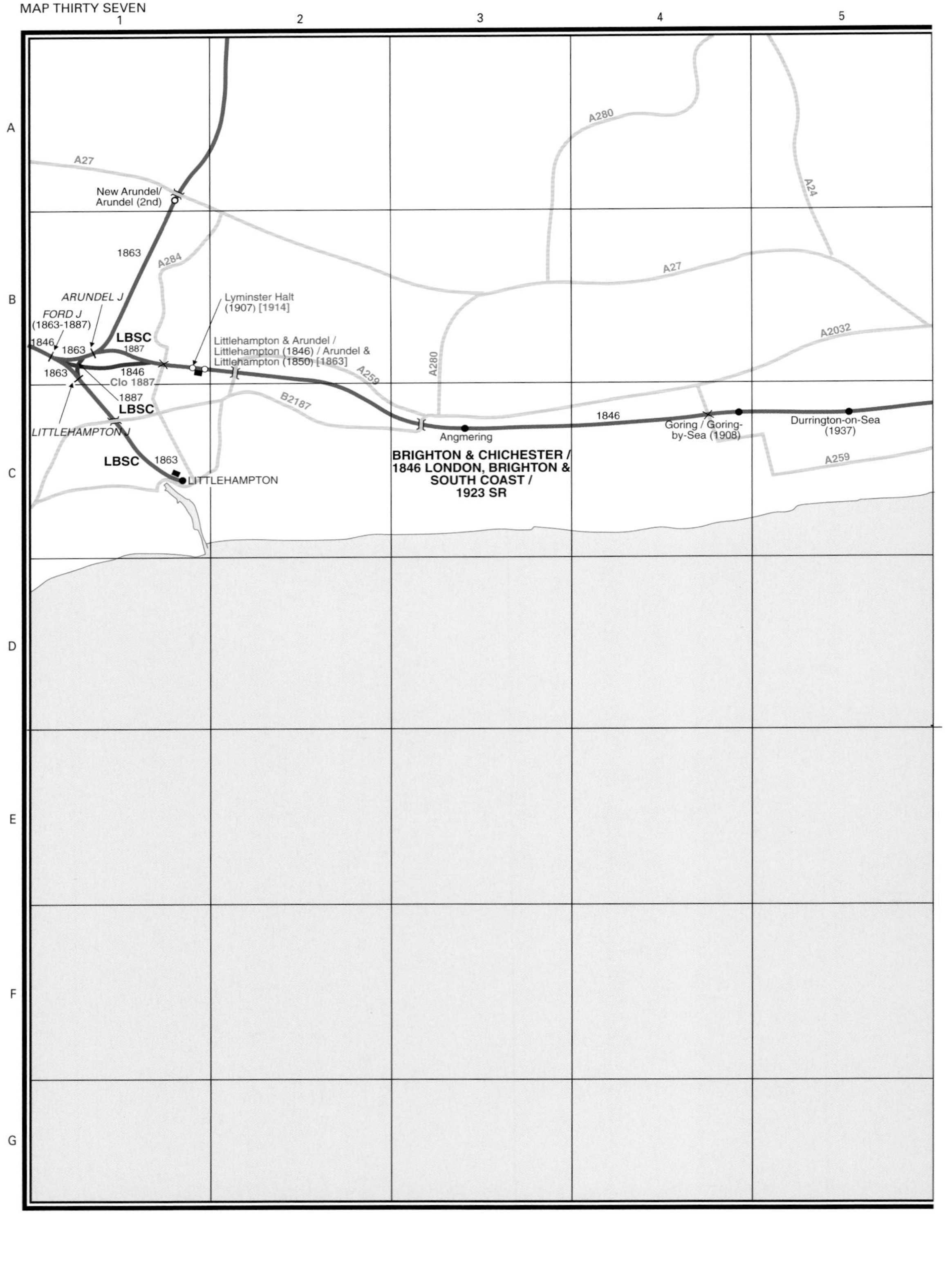

1 2 3 4 5

A B C D E F G

A27
A280
A24
A284
A2032
A259
B2187

New Arundel/
Arundel (2nd)

1863

ARUNDEL J

FORD J
(1863-1887)

1846
1863
1863
1846
1887
LBSC

Lyminster Halt
(1907) [1914]

Littlehampton & Arundel /
Littlehampton (1846) / Arundel &
Littlehampton (1850) [1863]

Clo 1887
1887
LBSC

LITTLEHAMPTON J

LBSC
1863
LITTLEHAMPTON

Angmering

1846

Goring / Goring-
by-Sea (1908)

Durrington-on-Sea
(1937)

**BRIGHTON & CHICHESTER /
1846 LONDON, BRIGHTON &
SOUTH COAST /
1923 SR**

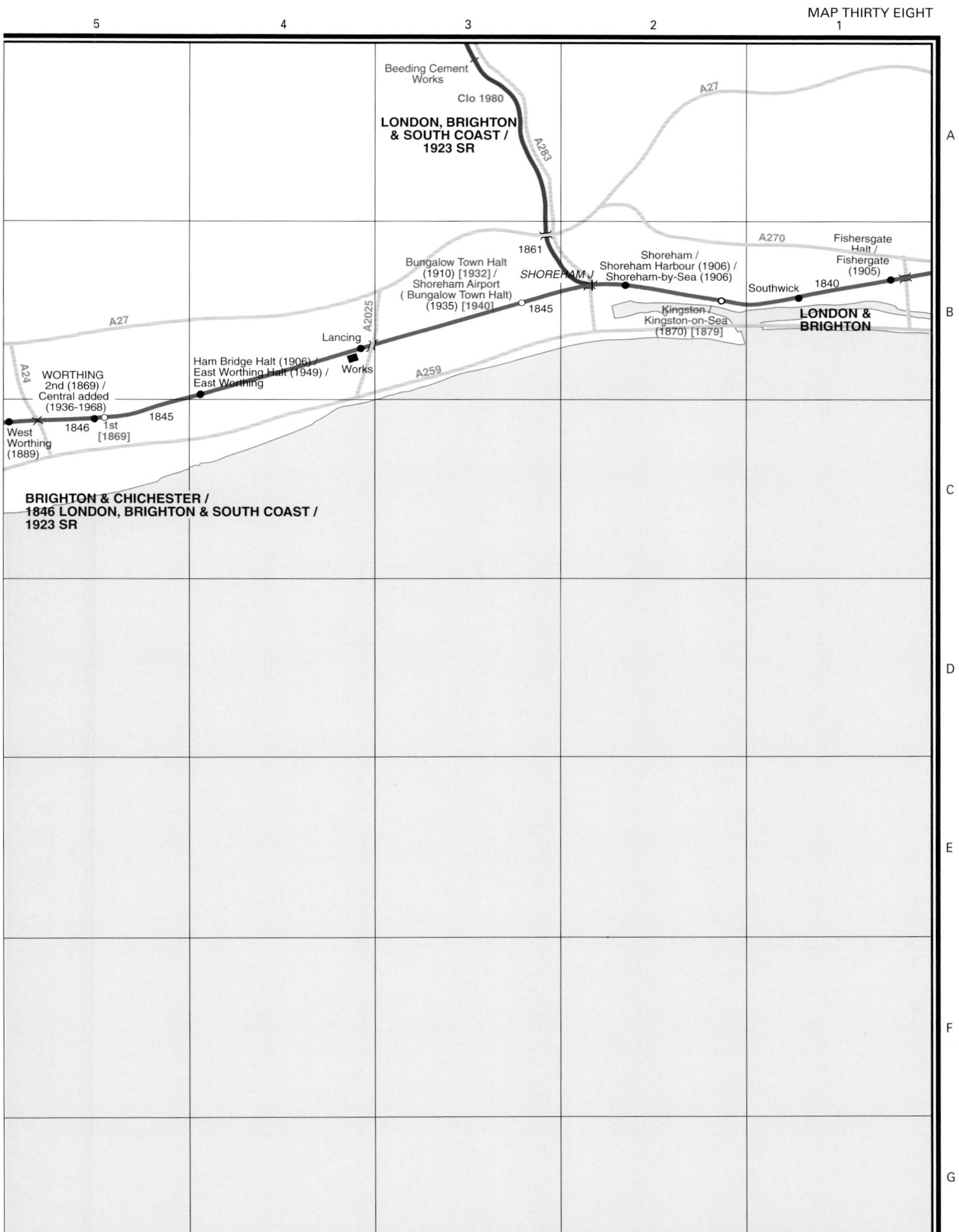

5
4
3
2
1
A
B
C
D
E
F
G
Beeding Cement Works
Clo 1980
LONDON, BRIGHTON & SOUTH COAST / 1923 SR
A27
A283
A270
Fishersgate Halt / Fishergate (1905)
1861
Shoreham / Shoreham Harbour (1906) / Shoreham-by-Sea (1906)
Bungalow Town Halt (1910) [1932] / Shoreham Airport (Bungalow Town Halt) (1935) [1940]
SHOREHAM J
Southwick
1840
1845
Kingston / Kingston-on-Sea (1870) [1879]
LONDON & BRIGHTON
A27
A2025
Lancing
Works
A24
WORTHING 2nd (1869) / Central added (1936-1968)
Ham Bridge Halt (1906) / East Worthing Halt (1949) / East Worthing
A259
1845
West Worthing (1889)
1846
1st [1869]
BRIGHTON & CHICHESTER / 1846 LONDON, BRIGHTON & SOUTH COAST / 1923 SR

MAP THIRTY NINE

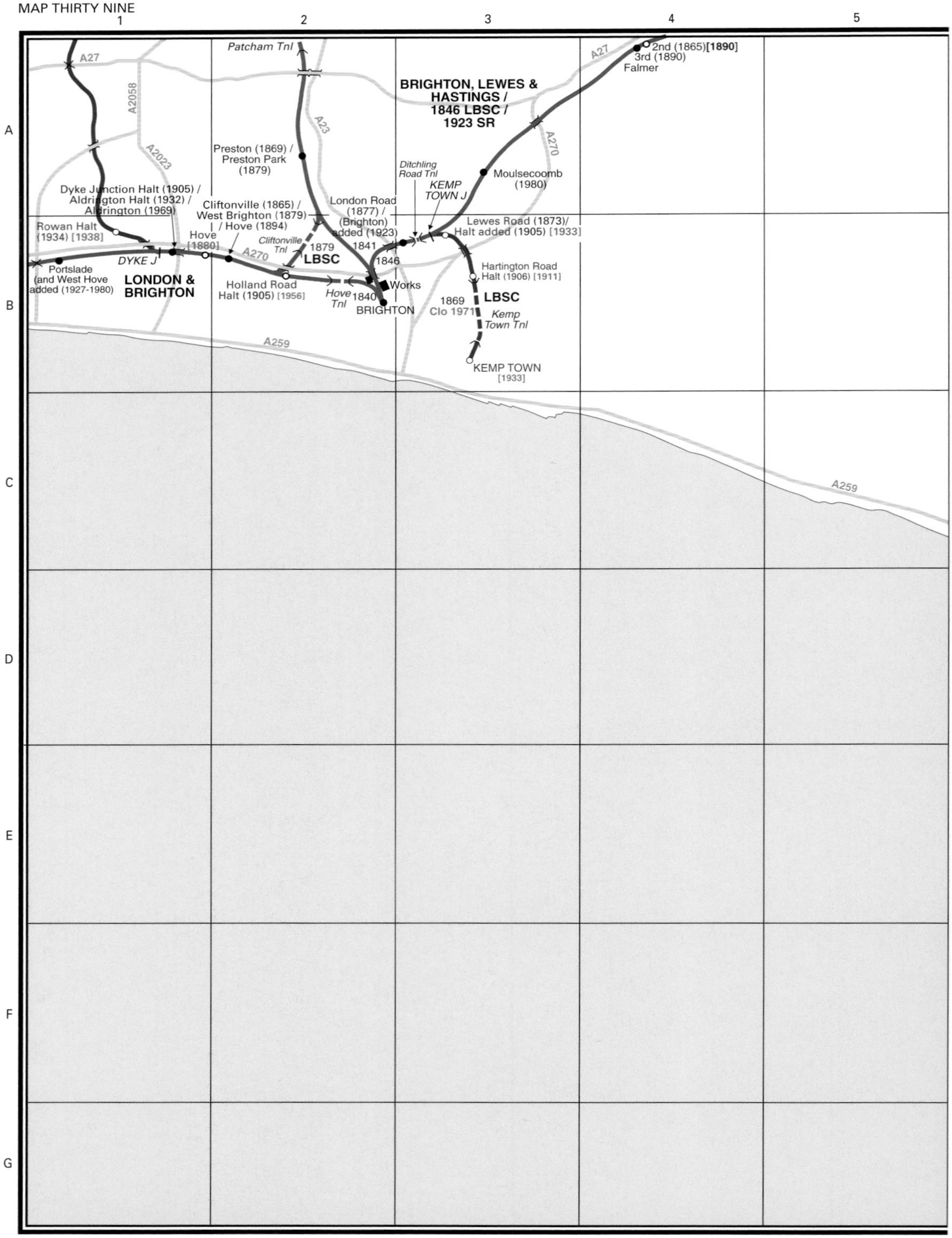

1 2 3 4 5

A B C D E F G

Patcham Tnl
A27
A2058
A23
BRIGHTON, LEWES & HASTINGS / 1846 LBSC / 1923 SR
2nd (1865)**[1890]**
3rd (1890)
Falmer
A270
A2023
Preston (1869) / Preston Park (1879)
Moulsecoomb (1980)
Ditchling Road Tnl
KEMP TOWN J
Dyke Junction Halt (1905) / Aldrington Halt (1932) / Aldrington (1969)
Cliftonville (1865) / West Brighton (1879) / Hove (1894)
London Road (1877) / (Brighton) added (1923)
Lewes Road (1873)/ Halt added (1905) [1933]
Rowan Halt (1934) [1938]
Hove [1880]
Cliftonville Tnl
1879
LBSC
1841
1846
Portslade (and West Hove added (1927-1980)
DYKE J
LONDON & BRIGHTON
Holland Road Halt (1905) [1956]
Hove Tnl
1840
Works
BRIGHTON
Hartington Road Halt (1906) [1911]
1869 Clo 1971
LBSC
Kemp Town Tnl
A259
KEMP TOWN [1933]
A259

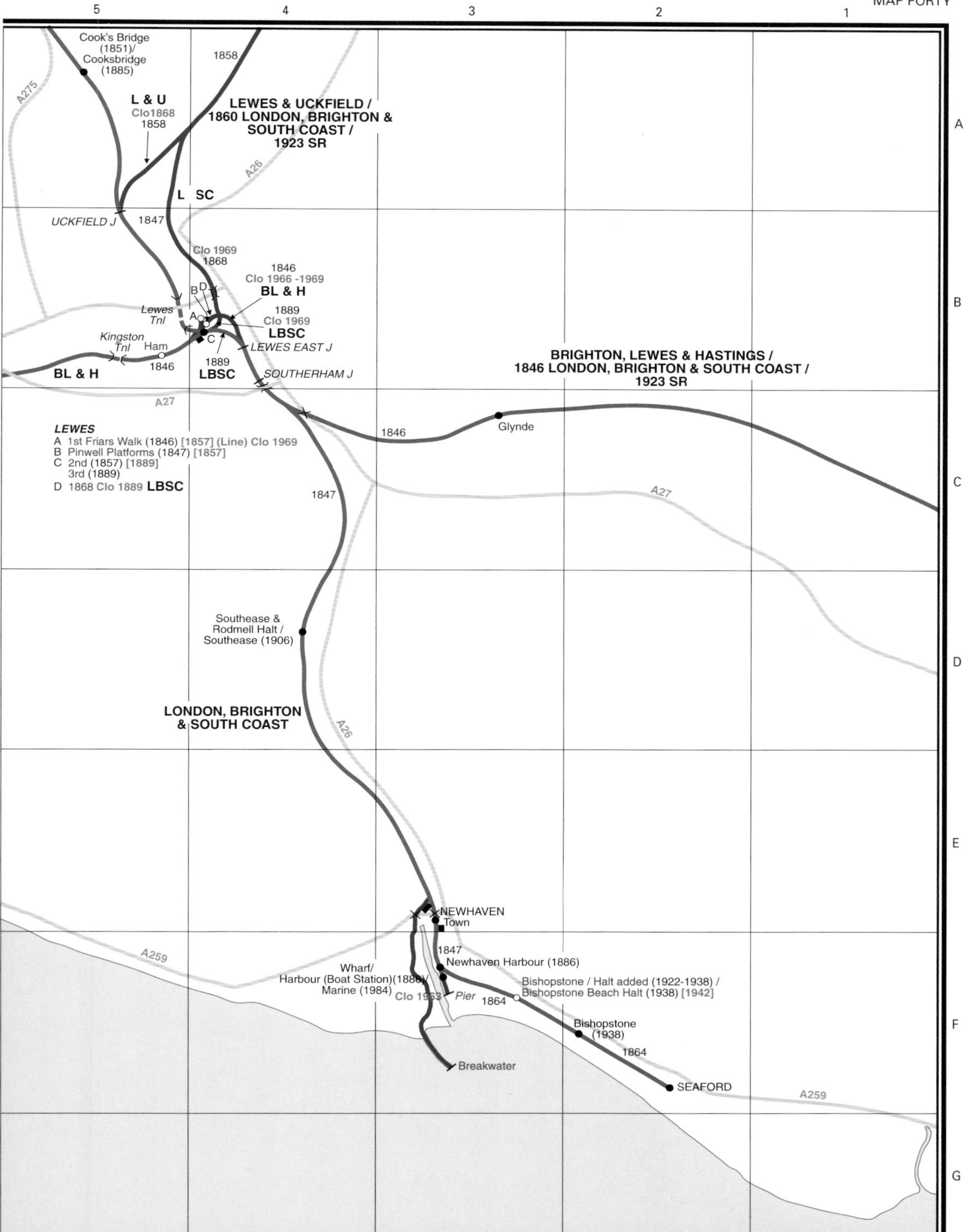
5
4
3
2
1
A
B
C
D
E
F
G
Cook's Bridge (1851)/ Cooksbridge (1885)
1858
L & U
Clo1868
1858
LEWES & UCKFIELD / 1860 LONDON, BRIGHTON & SOUTH COAST / 1923 SR
A275
A26
L SC
UCKFIELD J
1847
Clo 1969
1868
1846
Clo 1966 -1969
BL & H
1889
Clo 1969
LBSC
Lewes Tnl
Kingston Tnl
Ham
1846
1889
LBSC
LEWES EAST J
SOUTHERHAM J
BL & H
A27
BRIGHTON, LEWES & HASTINGS / 1846 LONDON, BRIGHTON & SOUTH COAST / 1923 SR
Glynde
1846
LEWES
A 1st Friars Walk (1846) [1857] (Line) Clo 1969
B Pinwell Platforms (1847) [1857]
C 2nd (1857) [1889]
3rd (1889)
D 1868 Clo 1889 LBSC
1847
A27
Southease & Rodmell Halt / Southease (1906)
LONDON, BRIGHTON & SOUTH COAST
A26
NEWHAVEN Town
1847
Newhaven Harbour (1886)
A259
Wharf/ Harbour (Boat Station)(1886)/ Marine (1984)
Clo 1963
Pier
1864
Bishopstone / Halt added (1922-1938) / Bishopstone Beach Halt (1938) [1942]
Bishopstone (1938)
1864
Breakwater
SEAFORD
A259

1 2 3 4 5

A B C D E F G

BRIGHTON, LEWES & HASTINGS / 1846 LONDON, BRIGHTON & SOUTH COAST / 1923 SR

LONDON, BRIGHTON & SOUTH COAST

Berwick

A22

1846

Clo 1881 1849

Clo 1968 1881

1st [1881] / 3rd (1986) Polegate

2nd (1881) [1986]

A27

1846 Clo 1969

1849

A27

West Ham & Pevensey / Pevensey & Westham (1851)

1846

STONE CROSS J

Stone Cross Halt (1905) [1935]

1871

LBSC

WILLINGDON J

A2270

Willingdon (1888) / Hampden Park (1903)

LONDON, BRIGHTON & SOUTH COAST

A259

A2021

1849

A2270

2nd

EASTBOURNE 1st

A259

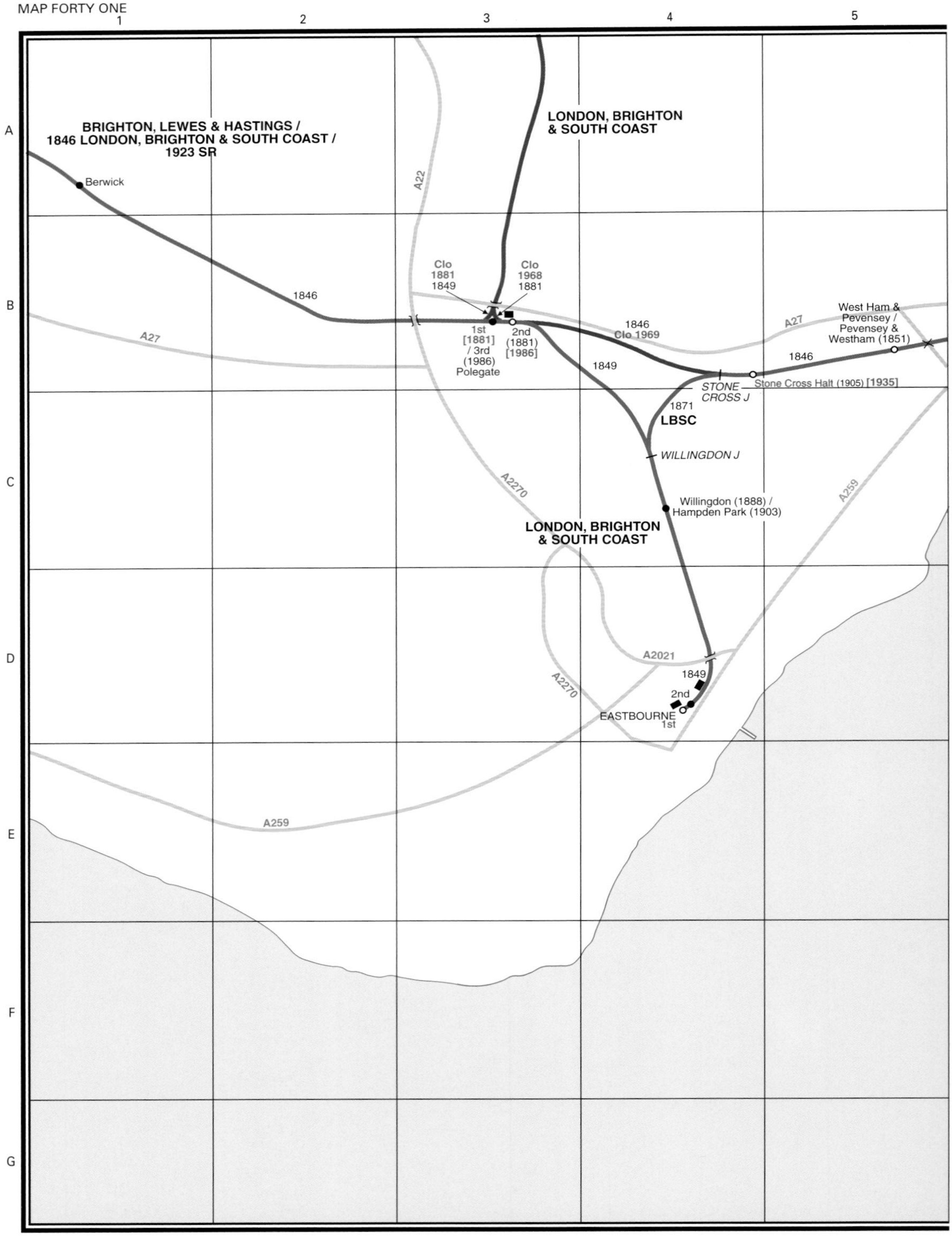

MAP INDEX AND GAZETTEER

Station	Map ref	Opened	Closed (passengers)	Closed (freight)
Abbots Court Pier	3C3	1915	n/a	1940
Adisham	7F2	22 July 1861	Open	7 May 1962*
Aldrington	39B1	3 September 1905	Open	n/a
Aldrington Halt	see Aldrington; renamed 5 May 1969			
Amberley	28F5	3 August 1863	Open	6 May 1963
Angmering	37C3	16 March 1846	Open	4 May 1964
APCM — Greenhithe	1A5	Unknown	n/a	1972
APCM — Stone	1A5	Unknown	n/a	1971
Appledore	24B5	13 February 1851	Open	27 May 1963
Ardingly Stone Terminal	20G5	Unknown	n/a	Open
Ardingly	20G5	3 September 1883	28 October 1963	2 April 1962
Arundel & Littlehampton	37B1	16 March 1846	1 September 1863	n/a
Arundel (first)	see Ford; renamed Ford 3 August 1863			
Arundel (second)	37A1	3 August 1863	Open	9 September 1963
Ash Town	7E4/8G5	1916	1 November 1948	31 October 1949+
Ashford (LC&DR)	14C3	1 July 1884	1 January 1899	Unknown
Ashford	14C2	1 December 1842	Open	Unknown
Ashurst	21B4	1 October 1888	Open	4 April 1960
Aylesford	11A2	18 June 1856	Open	18 April 1964*
Aylesham	7G2	1 July 1928	Open	n/a
Aylesham Halt	see Aylesham; renamed 5 May 1969			
Balcombe	19F2	12 July 1841	Open	14 September 1959
Barcombe (second)	31G2	1 August 1882	13 June 1955	13 June 1955
Barcombe Mills	31G2	18 October 1858	4 May 1969***	6 May 1963
Barcombe (first)	see Barcombe Mills; station renamed 1 January 1885			
Barham	16A5	4 July 1887	1 December 1940	1 October 1947
Barming	11B3	1 June 1874	Open	5 December 1960
Barnham	36B2	1 June 1864	Open	28 September 1964
Barnham Junction	see Barnham; name changed 7 July 1929			
Bat & Ball	9B5	2 June 1862	Open	25 May 1968*
Battle	33B5	1 January 1852	Open	2 October 1966
Bearsted & Thurnham	see Bearsted; known as Bearsted & Thurnham 1 July 1907 to June 1980			
Bearsted	11B5	1 July 1884	Open	7 October 1968
Beeding Cement Works	38A3	1896	n/a	26 March 1988
Bekesbourne	6E1	22 July 1861	Open	5 June 1961
Beltring & Branbridges Halt	see Beltring; renamed June 1980			
Beltring	11E1	1 September 1909	Open	5 June 1961
Beluncle Halt	3B4	July 1906	4 December 1961	n/a
Berwick	41A1	27 June 1846	Open	6 May 1963
Betteshanger Colliery	17B2	1924	n/a	1989
Bexhill	33E4	27 June 1846	Open	30 April 1962*
Bexhill Central	see Bexhill; renamed from Bexhill 9 July 1923; lost 'Central' suffix in 1960s			
Bexhill	see Bexhill West; renamed Bexhill-on-Sea 1920			
Bexhill West	33E4	1 June 1902	25 June 1964	9 September 1963
Bexhill-on-Sea	see Bexhill West; renamed 9 September 1923			
Biddenden	13E2	15 May 1905	4 January 1954	4 January 1954
Billingshurst	28A2	10 October 1859	Open	4 May 1964*
Birchington	see Birchington-on-Sea; renamed October 1878			
Birchington-on-Sea	8B5	5 October 1863	Open	4 June 1962
Bishopsbourne	6F1	1 July 1889	1 December 1940	1 October 1947
Bishopstone (first)	see Bishopstone Halt (first); renamed 1 August 1922			
Bishopstone Halt (first)	40F3	1 June 1864	26 September 1938	1 August 1922
Bishopstone (second)	40F2	26 September 1938	Open	n/a
Bishopstone Halt (second)	see Bishopstone (second); renamed 5 May 1969			
Bishopstone Beach Halt	40F3	6 April 1939	1 January 1942	n/a
Blean & Tyler Hill Halt	6C3	January 1908	1 January 1931	n/a
Bodiam**	23E3	2 February 1900	4 January 1954	12 June 1961
Bognor Regis	36D3	1 June 1864	Open	3 May 1971
Bognor	see Bognor Regis; renamed 1929			
Bognor	see Woodgate; name changed October 1846			
Borough Green & Wrotham	10B3	1 June 1874	Open	9 September 1968
Bosham	35B3	15 March 1847	Open	6 May 1963
Botolphs Bridge Halt**	15F3	16 July 1927	1936	n/a
Bramber	29G3	1 July 1861	7 March 1966	n/a
Brambledown Halt	5B2	March 1905	4 December 1950	n/a
Brasted Halt	9B2	7 July 1881	30 October 1961	30 October 1961
Brasted	see Brasted Halt; renamed 19 September 1955			
Bridge	6F1	1 July 1889	1 December 1940	1 October 1947
Brighton	39B2	11 May 1840	Open	Unknown
Brighton Central	see Brighton; suffix carried for period until 30 September 1935			
Broadstairs	8C1	5 October 1863	Open	3 June 1963
Brookgate — Aylesford Newsprint	11A2	Unknown	n/a	Open
Brookland Halt	25C5	7 December 1881	6 March 1967	n/a
Brookland	see Brookland Halt; renamed 1930			
Bungalow Town Halt	38B3	3 September 1905	1 January 1933	n/a
Burgess Hill	30C3	21 September 1841	Open	7 November 1966
Burmarsh Road Halt**	25A5/15G2	16 July 1927	1938*****	n/a
Buxted	31D5	3 August 1868	Open	2 April 1962
Camber Sands	24F4	13 July 1908	4 September 1939	4 September 1939
Canterbury (CW)	6C1	4 May 1830	6 April 1846	1848

KENT AND SUSSEX

Station	Map ref	Opened	Closed (passengers)	Closed (freight)
Canterbury East	6D2	9 July 1860	Open	19 September 1965
Canterbury	see Canterbury East; renamed 1 July 1899			
Canterbury	see Canterbury West; renamed1 July 1899			
Canterbury South	6E2	1 July 1889	1 December 1940	1 October 1947
Canterbury West	6D2	6 February 1846	Open	31 December 1986
Chalder	35D5	27 August 1897	19 January 1935	19 January 1935
Chartham	6E4	1859	Open	19 November 1962
Chatham	3D2	25 January 1858	Open	Unknown
Chatham Central	3D2	1 March 1892	1 October 1911	n/a
Chatham Dockyard	3C3	16 February 1877	n/a	1994
Chattenden	3B3	1875	31 December 1961	31 December 1961
Cheriton Arch	see Folkestone Central; renamed Radnor Park October 1886			
Cheriton Halt	16F5	1 May 1908	16 June 1947	n/a
Chestfield & Swalecliffe	6A3	6 July 1930	Open	n/a
Chestfield & Swalecliffe Halt	see Chestfield & Swalecliffe; renamed 5 May 1969			
Chevening Halt	9B2	16 April 1906	31 October 1961	n/a
Chichester (first)	35B5	8 June 1846	15 March 1847	n/a
Chichester (second)	35B5	15 March 1847	Open	n/a
Chichester (Selsey)	35B5	27 August 1897	19 January 1935	19 January 1935
Chilham	6F5	6 February 1846	Open	15 August 1966
Chislet Colliery	7C1	1918	n/a	July 1969
Chislet Colliery	7C1	1920	4 October 1971	n/a
Chislet Colliery Halt	see Chislet Colliery; renamed 5 May 1969			
Christ's Hospital	18F3	28 April 1902	Open	4 September 1961
Christ's Hospital, West Horsham	see Christ's Hospital; renamed post-1948			
Church Street	6A3	1830	1846	n/a
Cliffe	3B1	31 March 1882	4 December 1961	20 August 1962
Cliftonville	see Hove (second); renamed West Brighton 1 July 1879			
Clowes Wood	6B3	3 May 1830	1846	n/a
Cocking Halt	26D1	11 July 1881	8 July 1935	31 August 1953
Cocking	see Cocking Halt; renamed 23 May 1932			
Collington	33E4	1 June 1911	Open	n/a
Collington Halt	see Collington; renamed 5 May 1969			
Collington Wood Halt	33E4	11 September 1905	1 September 1906	n/a
Cooden Beach	33F3	11 September 1905	Open	n/a
Cooden Golf Halt	see Cooden Beach; renamed Cooden Halt by 1922			
Cooden Halt	see Cooden Beach; renamed 7 July 1935			
Cook's Bridge	see Cooksbridge; renamed May 1885			
Cooksbridge	40A5	January 1881	Open	2 October 1961
Cowden	21A5	1 October 1888	Open	4 April 1960
Cranbrook	23B4	4 September 1893	12 June 1961	12 June 1961
Crawley (first)	19C3	14 February 1848	29 July 1968	Unknown
Crawley (second)	19C3	29 July 1968	Open	n/a
Crowborough & Jarvis Brook	see Crowborough; renamed 1980			
Crowborough	21F3	3 August 1868	Open	5 August 1968
Crowhurst	33C5	1 June 1902	Open	5 June 1961
Cuxton	2E1	18 June 1856	Open	5 June 1961*
Dartford	1B4	30 July 1849	Open	1 May 1972
Deal	17B3	1 July 1847	Open	1 May 1972*
Denton Halt	2B3	July 1906	4 December 1961	n/a
Dixter Halt**	23E4	24 May 1981	Open	n/a
Doleham	34B3	1 July 1907	Open	6 February 1961
Doleham Halt	see Doleham; renamed 5 May 1969			
Dover Admiralty Pier	see Dover Western Docks; renamed Dover Marine 5 December 1918			
Dover Harbour (first)	17G1	1 November 1861	June 1863	n/a
Dover Harbour (second)	17G1	June 1863	10 July 1927	n/a
Dover Marine	see Dover Western Docks; renamed 15 May 1979			
Dover Prince of Wales Pier	17F2	1902	1909	n/a
Dover Priory	16G1	22 July 1861	Open	3 July 1961
Dover	see Dover Town; renamed December 1861			
Dover Town & Harbour	see Dover Harbour (second); renamed 1 July 1899			
Dover Town	16E1/17G1	7 February 1844	14 October 1914	11 August 1919
Dover Town (Priory)	see Dover Priory; renamed July 1863			
Dover Western Docks	17G1	18 January 1919	26 September 1994	Unknown
Drayton	36B5	8 June 1846	1 June 1930	9 September 1963
Dumpton Park	8D1	2 July 1926	Open	n/a
Dungeness	25G1	1 April 1883	4 July 1937	1952*
Dungeness Lighthouse	see Dungeness; renamed 21 March 1947 (after temporary closure for war since 30 June 1940)			
Dungeness Power Station	25F2	1965	n/a	Open
Dungeness**	25G1	August 1928	Open	n/a
Dunton Green & Riverhead	see Dunton Green; renamed1 July 1873			
Dunton Green	9B4	2 March 1868	Open	2 April 1962*
Durrington-on-Sea	37C5	4 July 1937	Open	n/a
Dyke Junction	see Aldrington; renamed Aldrington Halt 1932			
Dymchurch**	25B1	16 July 1927	Open	n/a
East Farleigh	11C3	25 September 1844	Open	3 July 1961
East Grinstead (first)	20B3	9 July 1855	1 October 1866	n/a
East Grinstead (second)	20B3	1 October 1866	15 October 1883	n/a
East Grinstead (third; High Level)	20B3	1 August 1882	2 January 1967	10 April 1967
East Grinstead (third; Low Level)	20B3	1 August 1882	Open	10 April 1967
East Malling	11B1	May 1913	Open	n/a
East Malling Halt	see East Malling; renamed 1959			
East Margate	see Margate East; renamed 1 July 1899			
East Minster-on-Sea	4E1/5A1	1902	4 December 1950	n/a
East Worthing Halt	38B4	3 September 1905	Open	n/a
Eastbourne (first)	41D4	14 May 1849	1866	n/a
Eastbourne (second)	41D4	1866	Open	28 September 1964
Eastchurch	5B2	1 August 1901	4 December 1950	4 December 1950
Eastry	7F5/17A1	1916	1 November 1948	1 March 1951
Eastry South	7F5/17A1	1925	1 November 1948	1 March 1951

Station	Map ref	Opened	Closed (passengers)	Closed (freight)
Ebbsfleet & Cliffsend Halt	8D3	May 1908	1 April 1933	n/a
Ebbsfleet International	2B5	14 November 2007	Open	n/a
Edenbridge	9F1	26 May 1842	Open	10 September 1962
Edenbridge	see Edenbridge Town; renamed 1 May 1896			
Edenbridge Town	9F1	2 January 1888	Open	7 October 1968
Elham	15B5	4 July 1887	1 December 1940	1 October 1947
Elmton	see Elvington; renamed date unknown			
Elsted	26C2	1 September 1864	7 February 1955	7 February 1955
Elvington	16A2	November 1925	1 November 1948	1 March 1951
Eridge	21D2	3 August 1868	Open	6 November 1961
Etchingham	22G5	1 September 1851	Open	3 December 1962
Ewell	see Kearsney; renamed 1 February 1869			
Eynsford	1F3	1 July 1862	Open	1 July 1862
Eythorne	16A2	1916	1 November 1948	8 August 1964*
Falmer (first)	30G2	8 August 1846	1 August 1865	n/a
Falmer (second)	39A4	39A4	1 August 1865	1890 n/a
Falmer (third)	39A4	1890	Open	4 September 1961
Farningham & Sutton	see Farningham Road; name changed to Farningham 1 August 1861; to Farningham Road September 1869; and to Farningham Road & Sutton-at-Hone in January 1872			
Farningham Road & Sutton-at-Hone	see Farningham Road; Sutton-at-Hone deleted 1980			
Farningham Road	1D4	3 December 1860	Open	20 May 1968*
Farningham	see Farningham Road; name changed to Farningham & Sutton 1 April 1861			
Faversham	5F4	25 January 1858	Open	16 August 1971*
Faversham Creek	5F4	12 April 1860	n/a	1964
Fawkham	see Longfield; name changed 12 June 1961			
Fay Gate	see Faygate; renamed 5 December 1953			
Faygate	19D5	14 February 1848	Open	6 November 1961
Ferry	35E5	1898	19 January 1935	19 January 1935
Ferry Siding	see Ferry; renamed 1911			
Fishbourne	35F4	1 April 1906	Open	n/a
Fishbourne Halt	see Fishbourne; suffix dropped 5 May 1969			
Fishersgate	38B1	3 September 1905	Open	
Fishersgate Halt	see Fishersgate; suffix dropped 5 May 1969			
Fittleworth	28D5	2 September 1889	7 February 1955	6 May 1963
Fletching & Sheffield Park	see Sheffield Park; renamed 1 January 1883			
Folkestone (first)	16F4	28 June 1843	18 December 1843	n/a
Folkestone (second)	see Folkestone East; various names from opening until renamed Folkestone East 10 September 1962			
Folkestone Central	16F4	1 September 1884	Open	n/a
Folkestone East	16F4	18 December 1843	6 September 1965++	xxxx
Folkestone Warren	16F3	1 June 1908	25 September 1939+++	n/a
Folkestone West	16F5	1 February 1881	Open	22 April 1968
Ford	36B1	8 June 1846	Open	8 October 1962
Ford (LBSCR)	see Ford; renamed Ford Junction 1 June 1864			
Ford (Sussex)	see Ford; renamed *c*1960			
Ford Junction	see Ford; renamed Ford (Sussex) 9 July 1923			
Forest Row	20D4	1 October 1866	2 January 1967	7 November 1966
Frant	22C1	1 September 1851	Open	3 September 1962
Frittenden Road	13D2	15 May 1905	4 January 1954	4 January 1954
Gillingham (Kent)	see Gillingham; renamed 9 July 1923			
Gillingham	3D3	1858	Open	4 May 1970*
Glynde	40C3	27 June 1846	Open	4 April 1960
Glyne Gap Halt	33E5	11 September 1905	1 October 1915	n/a
Golden Sands Halt	25B5	1951	17 September 1977	n/a
Golf Links	24F4	13 July 1895	4 September 1939	n/a
Goring	see Goring-by-Sea; name changed 1 April 1908			
Goring-by-Sea	37C4	16 March 1846	Open	7 May 1962
Goudhurst	22C5	1 October 1892	12 June 1961	12 June 1961
Grain — BP	4D5	1923	n/a	Open
Grain Crossing Halt	4D5	1 July 1906	4 September 1951	n/a
Grain	4D5	4 September 1951	4 December 1961	n/a
Grange Road	20E1	2 April 1860	2 January 1967	2 October 1961
Graveney Siding	6B5	Unknown	n/a	5 February 1962
Gravesend (SER)	see Gravesend; renamed Gravesend Central 1 July 1899			
Gravesend	2B3	30 July 1849	Open	6 November 1961
Gravesend Canal Basin	2B3	10 February 1845	30 July 1849	30 July 1849
Gravesend Central	see Gravesend; renamed 14 June 1965			
Gravesend	see Gravesend West; renamed Gravesend West Street 1 July 1899			
Gravesend West	2B3	10 May 1886	3 August 1953	25 May 1968
Gravesend West Street	see Gravesend West; renamed 26 September 1949			
Greatstone-on-Sea	see Greatstone-on-Sea Halt; renamed 14 June 1954			
Greatstone Dunes	see Greatstone Halt; also known as Greatstone-on-Sea and Greatstone			
Greatstone Halt	25D2	24 May 1928	November 1983	n/a
Greatstone-on-Sea Halt	25D1	4 July 1937	6 March 1967	n/a
Greenhithe	see Greenhithe for Bluewater; renamed post-2000			
Greenhithe for Bluewater	1B5	30 July 1849	Open	n/a
Groombridge*	21C3	1 October 1866	8 July 1985	7 October 1968
Grove Ferry & Upstreet	7C2	13 April 1846	3 January 1966	30 April 1960
Grove Ferry	see Grove Ferry & Upstreet; renamed 20 September 1954			
Grovehurst Paper Mill	12A1	Unopened	n/a	Open
Guildford Colliery	16B2	Unknown	n/a	Unopened
Hailsham	32G3	14 May 1849	9 September 1968	5 August 1968
Halling	2F1	1 March 1890	Open	4 September 1961*
Halling Cement Works	2F1	xxxx	n/a	xxxx
Ham	40B5	8 June 1846	1 November 1857	n/a
Ham Bridge Halt	see East Worthing Halt; renamed 1949			
Ham Street & Orlestone	see Ham Street; '& Orlestone' suffix carried 1 February 1897 to 1976			
Ham Street	14F3	13 February 1852	Open	4 December 1961
Hampden Park for Willingdon	see Hampden Park; renamed xxxx			
Hampden Park	41C4	1 January 1888	Open	28 September 1964
Harrietsham	12F3	1 July 1884	Open	1 May 1961

KENT AND SUSSEX

Station	Map ref	Opened	Closed (passengers)	Closed (freight)
Hartfield	21C5	1 October 1866	2 January 1967	7 May 1962
Hartington Road Halt	39B3	1 January 1906	1 June 1911	n/a
Harty Road Halt	5B3	March 1905	4 December 1950	n/a
Hassocks	30E4	21 September 1881	Open	7 November 1966
Hassocks Gate	see Hassocks; name changed 1 October 1881			
Hastings & St Leonards	see St Leonards (West Marina); renamed St Leonards 13 February 1851			
Hastings	34E4	13 February 1851	Open	3 May 1971
Hawkhurst	23B4	4 September 1893	12 June 1961	12 June 1961
Haywards Heath	30A3	12 July 1841	Open	11 May 1970*
Headcorn	13C2	31 August 1842	Open	2 April 1962
Headcorn Junction	13C2	15 May 1905	4 January 1954	4 January 1954
Heathfield	32B3	5 April 1880	13 June 1965	5 August 1968
Hellingly	32F3	5 April 1880	14 June 1965	28 September 1964
Hellingly Hospital	32F3	1903	1931	1959
Henfield	29D3	1 July 1861	7 March 1966	7 May 1962
Herne Bay & Harrington-on-Sea	see Herne Bay; renamed March 1951			
Herne Bay	6A1	13 July 1861	Open	7 October 1968
Hever	9G2	1 October 1888	Open	26 November 1955
High Halden Road	13F3	15 May 1905	4 January 1954	4 January 1954
High Halstow Halt	3B3	July 1906	4 December 1961	n/a
High Rocks Halt**	21B2	1 June 1907	5 May 1952	n/a
Hildenborough	10E5	1 May 1868	Open	5 December 1960
Hodson's Siding	23F1	Unknown	n/a	1 January 1970
Hoe Farm Halt	35D5	27 August 1897	20 January 1935	20 January 1935
Holiday Camp (for St Mary's in the Marsh & Dymchurch Bay)		see Jefferstone Lane; renamed Holiday Camp Halt		
Holiday Camp Halt	see Jefferstone Lane; renamed St Mary's Bay 1946; usually known as 'Jesson' prior to 1946			
Holland Road	39B1	n/a	n/a	14 June 1971
Holland Road Halt	39B2	3 September 1905	7 May 1956	n/a
Hollingbourne	12F4	1 July 1884	Open	15 May 1961
Hoo Staff Halt	2B1	1956	Unadvertised staff halt	
Hope Mill	see Goudhurst; renamed 1 December 1892			
Horam	32D3	5 April 1880	13 June 1965	6 May 1963
Horeham Road & Waldron	see Horam; renamed Waldron & Horeham Road 1 April 1900			
Horsham (first)	18E4	5 April 1880	10 October 1959	n/a
Horsham (second)	18E4	10 October 1859	Open	4 May 1970
Horsmonden	22B5	1 October 1892	12 June 1961	12 June 1961
Horsted Keynes**	20F4	1 August 1882	28 October 1963	5 March 1962
Hothfield Halt	14B3	1 July 1884	2 November 1959	22 February 1964*
Hothfield	see Hothfield Halt; renamed 13 August 1937			
Hothfield Stone Terminal	14B3	Unknown	n/a	Open
Hove & West Brighton	see Hove (second); renamed 1 July 1895			
Hove (first)	39B1	11 May 1840	1 March 1880	Renamed Holland Road 1 July 1895
Hove (second)	39B2	1 October 1865	Open	4 November 1968
Hunston	35C5	27 August 1897	19 January 1935	19 January 1935
Hythe (Kent)	see Hythe; renamed from Hythe 21 September 1929; renamed Hythe for Sandgate November 1931 and to Hythe on 2 July 1939.			
Hythe (RH&DR)**	15E4	16 July 1927	Open	n/a
Hythe	15E5	10 October 1874	3 December 1951	3 December 1951
Ifield	19C4	1 June 1907	Open	n/a
Ifield Halt	see Ifield; renamed 6 July 1930			
Isfield**	31F3	18 October 1858	4 May 1969***	10 September 1962*
Jackwood Springs	21B1	20 September 1845	25 November 1846	n/a
Jefferstone Lane**	25B1	16 July 1927	Open	n/a
Junction Road Halt & Siding	23F4	2 February 1900	4 January 1954	12 June 1961
Kearsney	16C2	1 August 1862	Open	4 September 1961
Kemp Town	39B3	2 August 1869	2 January 1933	28 June 1971
Kemsing	10B5	1 June 1874	Open	31 October 1960
Kemsley	12A2	1 January 1927	Open	n/a
Kemsley Down**	12A1	28 March 1970	Open	n/a
Kemsley Halt	see Kemsley			
Keymer Junction (first)	30C3	1854	1 January 1862	n/a
Keymer Junction (second)	30C3	1 January 1862	1 November 1883	n/a
Keymer Junction (third)	see Wivelsfield; renamed 1 July 1896			
King's Ferry Bridge North Halt	1 March 1922	1 November 1923	n/a	
King's Ferry Bridge South Halt	see Swale Halt (first); renamed 1 June 1929			
Kingscote**	20C4	1 August 1882	13 June 1955	13 June 1955
Kingsnorth	3C3	1915	n/a	1940
Kingston	see Kingston-on-Sea; renamed 1 December 1870			
Kingston-on-Sea	38B2	12 May 1840	1 April 1879	7 October 1968
Knowlton Halt	7G4	1916	1 November 1948	31 October 1949+
Lade Halt	25E1	24 May 1928	November 1983	n/a
Lade	see Lade Halt; renamed 1947			
Lancing	38B4	24 November 1845	Open	3 April 1967
Lavant	35A5	11 July 1881	8 July 1935	Unknown
Leigh	9F5	1 September 1911	Open	n/a
Leigh Halt	see Leigh; renamed Lyghe Halt 1917			
Lenham	12F2	1 July 1884	Open	6 January 1969
Lewes (first)	40B4	1 November 1857	4 March 1889	n/a
Lewes (second)	40B4	4 March 1889	xxxx	
Lewes (Friars Walk)	40B4	8 June 1847	1 November 1857	
Lewes Pinwell Platforms	40B4	1 October 1847	1 November 1857	n/a
Lewes Road Halt	39B3	1 September 1873	2 January 1933	n/a
Lewes Road	see Lewes Road Halt; renamed 1905			
Leysdown	5B4	1 August 1901	4 December 1950	4 December 1950
Littlehampton & Arundel	see Arundel & Littlehampton; renamed Littlehampton (first) 8 June 1846			
Littlehampton (first)	see Arundel & Littlehampton; renamed May 1850.			
Littlehampton (second)	37C1	17 August 1863	Open	18 May 1970*
Littlehaven	18E5	1 June 1907	Open	n/a
Littlehaven Crossing Halt	see Littlehaven; renamed Littlehaven Halt December 1907			

Station	Map ref	Opened	Closed (passengers)	Closed (freight)
Littlehaven Halt	see Littlehaven; renamed 5 May 1969			
Littlestone Holiday Camp	see Romney Sands; renamed Maddieson's Camp			
Littlestone	see New Romney; station originally New Romney but called Littlestone subsequently; reverted 1946			
Lodge Hill	3B3	1905	31 December 1961	31 December 1961
London Road (Brighton)	39B2	1 October 1877	Open	n/a
London Road	see London Road (Brighton); renamed 9 July 1923			
Longfield	2D5	June 1872	Open	7 May 1962
Longfield Halt	2D5	1 July 1913	3 May 1953	n/a
Lullingstone	1E3	Completed 1939 but never opened		
Lutnor	3B3	1875	31 December 1961	31 December 1961
Lydd	see Lydd Town; renamed 4 July 1937			
Lydd Camp	25F4	1883	n/a	1927
Lydd Town	25E3	7 December 1881	6 March 1967	4 October 1971
Lydd-on-Sea Halt	25F1	4 July 1937	6 March 1967	n/a
Lydd-on-Sea	see Lydd-on-Sea Halt; renamed 20 September 1954			
Lyghe Halt	see Leigh; renamed *c*1960			
Lyminge	15C5	4 July 1887	16 June 1947	1 October 1947
Lyminster Halt	37B1	1 August 1907	September 1914	n/a
Lyons Crossing Halt	see Ifield; renamed Ifield Halt July 1907			
Maddieson's Camp	see Romney Sands; renamed 1981			
Maidstone Barracks	11B4	1874	Open	n/a
Maidstone East	11B4	1 June 1874	Open	13 September 1965
Maidstone Road	see Paddock Wood; renamed 24 September 1844			
Maidstone	see Maidstone East; renamed 1 July 1899			
Maidstone	see Maidstone West; renamed 1 July 1899			
Maidstone West	11C4	25 September 1844	Open	Unknown
Mainland Car Terminal	4E3	Unknown	n/a	Open
Malling	see West Malling; renamed 23 May 1949			
Manston Camp	8C3	28 July 1918	n/a	c1925
Marden	11G3	31 August 1842	Open	3 September 1962
Margate & Cliftonville	see Margate; renamed from Margate December 1880 and to Margate West 1 July 1899			
Margate (SER)	see Margate Sands			
Margate	8B3	5 October 1863	Open	1 November 1972
Margate East	8B2	1870	4 May 1953	n/a
Margate Goods	8B3	Unknown	n/a	November 1976
Margate Sands	8B3	1 December 1846	2 July 1926	20 December 1926
Margate West	see Margate; renamed 11 July 1926			
Martin Mill	17E2	Open	4 September 1961	
Mayfield	21G1	1 September 1880	13 June 1965	6 May 1963
Meopham	2D3	6 May 1861	Open	2 April 1962
Middle Stoke Halt	3A5	July 1906	4 December 1961	n/a
Midhurst (first)	27B1	15 October 1866	11 July 1881	n/a
Midhurst (LSWR)	27B1	1 September 1864	13 July 1925	13 July 1925
Midhurst (second)	27C1	11 July 1881	7 February 1955	12 October 1964
Mill Pond Halt (first)	35E5	15 October 1910	May 1911	n/a
Mill Pond Halt (second)	35E5	9 July 1928	19 January 1935	
Milton Range Halt	2B2	July 1906	17 July 1932	n/a
Milton Road Halt	2B3	August 1906	1 May 1915	n/a
Minster (Sheppey)	see Minster-on-Sea; renamed 1 May 1906			
Minster (Thanet)	see Minster; renamed *c*1971			
Minster	7B5/8D4	13 April 1846	Open	9 September 1963*
Minster Junction (Thanet)	see Minster; renamed Minster (Thanet) 7 May 1945			
Minster Junction	see Minster; renamed from Minster on 1 January 1852 and renamed Minster Junction (Thanet) on 1 August 1901			
Minster (Sheppey)	see Minster-on-Sea; renamed 1 May 1906			
Minster-on-Sea	4E2/5A1	1 August 1901	4 December 1950	4 December 1950
MoD Sound Barrier	25E2	1933	n/a	1952
Moulescomb	39A1	1980	Open	n/a
Mountfield — British Gypsum	33A3	1876	n/a	Open
Mountfield Halt	33A4	1923	6 October 1969	n/a
New Arundel	see Arundel (second); renamed date unknown			
New Barcombe	see Barcombe; station renamed 1 January 1885			
New Brompton (Gillingham)	see Gillingham; renamed Gillingham 1 October 1912 and Gillingham (Kent) 9 July 1923			
New Brompton	see Gillingham; renamed New Brompton (Gillingham) May 1886			
New Hythe	11A2	9 December 1929	Open	n/a
New Hythe Halt	see New Hythe; renamed 1936			
New Romney & Littlestone	see New Romney & Littlestone-on-Sea; renamed October 1888			
New Romney & Littlestone-on-Sea	25D2	19 June 1884	6 March 1967	18 April 1964
New Romney**	25D2	16 July 1927	Open	n/a
Newhaven Breakwater	40F3	1880	n/a	10 August 1963
Newhaven Harbour	40F3	17 May 1886	Open	n/a
Newhaven Harbour (Boat Station)	see Newhaven Marine; renamed 14 May 1984			
Newhaven Marine	40F3	17 May 1886	Open	n/a
Newhaven Town	40E3	6 December 1847	Open	31 August 1987
Newhaven Wharf	40F3	6 December 1847	17 May 1886	n/a
Newhaven	see Newhaven Town; renamed July 1864			
Newick & Chailey	31E1	17 March 1958	13 June 1955	
Newington	12A3	1 August 1862	Open	1 October 1962
Normans Bay	33F2	11 September 1905	Open	n/a
Normans Bay Halt	see Normans Bay; suffix dropped 5 May 1969			
Northfleet (Blue Circle)	2B4	17 July 1970	n/a	1990s
Northfleet	2B4	1849	Open	9 September 1968
Northiam**	23E1	2 February 1900	4 January 1954	12 June 1961
Nutbourne	35B2	1 April 1906	Open	n/a
Nutbourne Halt	see Nutbourne; suffix dropped 5 May 1969			
Ore	34D4	1 January 1888	Open	1 May 1973
Otford	9A5	1 August 1882	Open	7 May 1962
Otford Junction	9A5	1 June 1874	1 November 1880	n/a
Otney	see Otford Junction (the station was known by both names)			

Station	Map ref	Opened	Closed (passengers)	Closed (freight)
Paddock Wood	10F1	31 August 1842	Open	3 January 1966*
Partridge Green	29C3	1 July 1861	7 March 1966	7 May 1962
Penshurst	9F4	26 May 1842	Open	9 September 1963
Petworth	27C4	10 October 1859	7 February 1955	23 May 1966
Pevensey	see Pevensey & Westham; known as Pevensey November 1851 to 1 January 1890			
Pevensey & Westham	41B5	27 June 1846	Open	4 September 1961
Pevensey Bay	33F1	11 September 1905	Open	n/a
Pevensey Bay Halt	see Pevensey Bay; suffix dropped 5 May 1969			
Pevensey Sluice	see Normans Bay; renamed Normans Bay Halt 1905			
Pluckley	19C5	1 December 1842	Open	2 September 1965
Plumpton	30D1	June 1863	Open	6 May 1963
Poison Cross Halt & Siding	7F5/17A1	1925	1 November 1928	1 January 1950
Polegate (first)	41B3	27 June 1846	3 October 1881	n/a
Polegate (second)	41B3	3 October 1881	25 May 1986	5 August 1968
Polegate (third)	41B3	25 May 1986	Open	n/a
Port Victoria	4D4	11 September 1882	11 June 1951	n/a
Portslade	39B	12 May 1840	Open	4 November 1968
Portslade & West Hove	see Portslade; called Portslade until April 1927 and after 1980			
Preston Park	39A2	1 November 1869	Open	n/a
Preston	see Preston Park; renamed 1 July 1879			
Prince of Wales Halt**	15F4	16 July 1927****	1928	n/a
Pulborough	28C4	10 October 1859	Open	5 September 1966
Queenborough	4E3	19 July 1860	Open	16 August 1971*
Queenborough Pier	4E3	15 May 1876	1 March 1923	1939
Queenborough Wharf	4E4	1863	1939	Open
Radnor Park	see Folkestone Central; renamed 1 June 1895			
Rainham & Newington	see Rainham; renamed 1 August 1862			
Rainham	3E4/12A5	25 January 1858	Open	2 April 1962
Ramsgate & St Lawrence-on-Sea	see Ramsgate Harbour; renamed 1 July 1899			
Ramsgate (first)	see Ramsgate Town; renamed 1 July 1899			
Ramsgate (second)	see Ramsgate Harbour; renamed Ramsgate & St Lawrence-on-Sea June 1871			
Ramsgate (third)	8D2	2 July 1926	Open	xxxx
Ramsgate Harbour	8D1	5 October 1863	2 July 1926	2 July 1926
Ramsgate Town	8D1	13 April 1846	2 July 1926	2 July 1926
Richborough Castle Halt	8F4	19 June 1933	11 September 1939	n/a
Richborough Port	8F3	1925	n/a	1 January 1950
Richborough Power Station	8E3	Unknown	n/a	1989
Ridham Dock	4G3	1919	n/a	Open
Ridham Dock Halt	see Swale Halt (first); renamed King's Ferry Bridge South Halt 1 March 1922 (station closed 1919 to 1 March 1922)			
Robertsbridge	23F5	1 September 1851	Open	10 June 1963
Rochester & Strood	see Rochester Bridge; renamed Rochester Bridge (Strood) March 1892			
Rochester (G&R)	3D1	10 February 1845	13 December 1846	13 December 1846
Rochester	3D2	1 March 1892	Open	30 September 1988
Rochester Bridge (Strood)	see Rochester Bridge; renamed January 1905			
Rochester Bridge	3D1	3 December 1860	1 January 1917	n/a
Rochester Central	3D2	20 July 1891	1 October 1911	5 September 1988
Rochester Common	see Rochester Central; renamed December 1901			
Rochester	see Rochester Central; renamed Rochester Common 1 july 1899			
Roffey Crossing Halt	see Roffey Road Halt; renamed July 1907			
Roffey Road Halt	18D5	1 June 1907	1 January 1937	n/a
Rogate	26B3	1 September 1864	7 February 1955	7 February 1955
Rolvenden**	13G3	2 April 1900	4 January 1954	12 June 1961
Roman Road (Woodnesborough)	7E5/8G4	1925	1 November 1928	1 January 1950
Roman Road, Woodnesborough	see Roman Road (Woodnesborough); renamed July 1931			
Romney Sands**	25E2	*c*1930	Open	n/a
Rosherville	see Rosherville Halt; renamed 17 February 1928			
Rosherville Halt	2B4	10 May 1886	16 July 1933	n/a
Rotherfield & Mark Cross	21F2	1 September 1880	13 June 1965	8 October 1962
Rotherfield	see Crowborough; renamed Crowborough 1 August 1880 and Crowborough & Jarvis Brook 1 May 1897			
Rotherfield	see Rotherfield & Mark Cross; renamed 1 November 1901			
Rowan Halt	39B1	18 December 1933	1 January 1939	n/a
Rowfant	19C1	9 July 1855	2 January 1967	7 August 1961*
Rudgwick	18D1	November 1856	14 June 1965	2 April 1962
Rusper Road Crossing Halt	see Littlehaven; renamed Littlehaven Crossing Halt July 1907			
Rye (R&C)	24E3	13 July 1895	4 September 1939	4 September 1939
Rye	24E3	13 February 1851	Open	9 September 1963
Rye Harbour	24F4	March 1854	n/a	1962 (CHECK - 1960 on maps)
St Lawrence (Pegwell Bay)	8D2	October 1864	3 April 1916	n/a
St Leonards, Bulverhythe	34E5	27 June 1846	7 November 1846	n/a
St Leonards (Warrior Square)	34E4	13 February 1851	Open	n/a
St Leonards (West Marina) (first)	34E5	7 November 1846	1882	n/a
St Leonards (West Marina) (second)	34E5	1882	10 July 1867	26 November 1962*
St Leonards	see St Leonards (Warrior Square); renamed 5 December 1870			
St Leonards	see St Leonards (West Marina); renamed 5 December 1870			
St Mary's Bay	see Jefferstone Lane; renamed 1981			
Salehurst Halt	23F4	1929	4 January 1954	12 June 1961
Sandgate	15E5	10 October 1874	1 April 1931	1 April 1931
Sandling	15E4	1 January 1888	Open 4 February 1963	
Sandling for Hythe	see Sandling; renamed 12 May 1980			
Sandling Junction	see Sandling; renamed 3 December 1951			
Sandwich	8G3	1 July 1847	Open	7 October 1963
Sandwich Road	7E5/8G4	1925	1 November 1928	1 January 1950
Seaford	40F2	1 June 1864	Open	4 May 1964
Selham	27C3	1 July 1872	7 February 1955	6 May 1963
Selling	5G5	3 December 1860	Open	5 November 1962
Selsey	35F5	27 August 1897	19 January 1935	19 January 1935
Selsey Beach	35F5	1 August 1898	October 1904	n/a
Selsey Bridge	35F5	27 August 1897	19 January 1935	n/a

Station	Map ref	Opened	Closed (passengers)	Closed (freight)
Selsey Golf Links Platform	35F5	1897	August 1914	n/a
Selsey Town	see Selsey; renamed 1911			
Seven Oaks	see Sevenoaks; renamed Sevenoaks April 1869 and Sevenoaks (Tubs Hill) 1 August 1869			
Sevenoaks (Bat & Ball)	see Bat & Ball; renamed 5 June 1950			
Sevenoaks (Tubs Hill) & Riverhead	see Sevenoaks; renamed Sevenoaks (Tubs Hill) 1880 to 1890 and after July 1901			
Sevenoaks (Tubs Hill)	see Sevenoaks; renamed Sevenoaks (Tubs Hill) & Riverhead 1 July 1873; station reverted to Sevenoaks (Tubs Hill) between 1880 and 1890 and again after July 1901; finally renamed Sevenoaks 5 June 1950			
Sevenoaks Junction	see Swanley Junction (first); renamed 1 January 1871			
Sevenoaks	see Bat & Ball; renamed Sevenoaks (Bat & Ball) 1 August 1869			
Shakespeare Cliff Halt	16E1	2 June 1913	Open++	n/a
Sharnal Street	3B3	31 March 1882	4 December 1961	20 August 1962*
Sheerness-on-Sea	4D3	1 June 1883	Open	Unknown
Sheerness	see Sheerness Dockyard; renamed 1 June 1883			
Sheerness Dockyard	4D3	16 April 1883	2 January 1922	Open
Sheerness East	4E2	1 August 1901	4 December 1950	4 December 1950
Sheffield Park**	31C1	1 August 1882	17 March 1958	13 June 1955
Shepherd's Well	16B3	22 July 1861	Open	10 June 1963*
Shepherd's Well** (EK)	16B3	1916	1 November 1948	1 March 1951
Shoreham (Kent)	1G3	2 June 1862	Open	7 May 1962
Shoreham Airport (Bungalow Town Halt)	38B31 July 1935	15 July 1940	n/a	
Shoreham Harbour	see Shoreham-by-Sea; renamed 1 October 1906			
Shoreham	see Shoreham (Kent); name changed 9 September 1923			
Shoreham	see Shoreham-by-Sea; renamed Shoreham Harbour 1 July 1906			
Shoreham-by-Sea	38B2	12 May 1840	Open	5 July 1965
Shorncliffe & Sandgate	see Shorncliffe Camp (first); renamed from Shorncliffe Camp 1 December 1863 and reverted 1 October 1874			
Shorncliffe Camp (first)	16F5	1 November 1863	1 February 1882	
Shorncliffe Camp (second)	see Folkestone West; renamed Shorncliffe 2 July 1926			
Shorncliffe	see Folkestone West; renamed 10 September 1962			
Sidlesham	35E5	27 August 1897	19 January 1935	19 January 1935
Sidley	33E4	1 June 1902	15 June 1964	9 September 1963
Singleton	26F1	11 July 1881	8 July 1935	31 August 1953
Sittingbourne & Milton Regis	see Sittingbourne; renamed 4 May 1970			
Sittingbourne & Milton	see Sittingbourne; renamed from Sittingbourne 1 July 1899 and to Sittingbourne & Milton Regis May 1908			
Sittingbourne	12B2	25 January 1858	Open	5 July 1976*
Sittingbourne (S&K)**	12B2	28 March 1970	Open	n/a
Sittingbourne Paper Mill	12B1	1906	n/a	Unknown
Slinfold	18E2	2 October 1865	14 June 1965 May 1962	
Smeeth	15D1	October 1852	4 January 1954	18 April 1964
Snailham Crossing Halt	see Snailham Halt; renamed 1909			
Snailham Halt	24F1/34A2	1 July 1907	2 February 1959	n/a
Snodland	2G1	18 June 1856	Open	10 June 1963
Snowdown & Nonington Halt	see Snowdown; renamed June 1980			
Snowdown	16A3	1914	Open	n/a
Snowdown Colliery	16A3	November 1912	n/a	1987
Snowdown for Nonington	see Snowdown; renamed 12 May 1980			
Sole Street	2D3	1 February 1861	Open	19 April 1965
South Canterbury	see Canterbury South; renamed xxxx			
South Street Halt	6A3	1 June 1911	1 January 1931	n/a
Southbourne	35B1	1 April 1906	Open	n/a
Southbourne Halt	see Southbourne; suffix dropped 5 May 1969			
Southease & Rodmell Halt	see Southease; renamed 12 May 1980			
Southease	40D4	1 September 1906	Open	n/a
Southfleet	2C5	10 May 1886	3 May 1953	11 June 1962
Southwater	18G4	16 September 1861	7 March 1966	7 May 1962
Southwick	38B1	12 May 1840	Open	n/a
Staple	7E4	1916	1 November 1948	1 March 1951
Staplehurst	11G5	31 August 1842	Open	4 October 1971
Steyning	29F2	1 July 1861	7 March 1966	7 May 1962
Stoke Junction Halt	3A5	17 July 1932	4 December 1961	n/a
Stone Cross Halt	41B4	11 September 1905	7 July 1935	n/a
Stone Crossing	1B5	2 November 1908	Open	n/a
Stone Crossing Halt	see Stone Crossing; suffix dropped 5 May 1969			
Stonegate	22G3	1 September 1851	Open	6 November 1961
Stonehall & Lydden Halt	16C2	1914	5 April 1954	n/a
Strood (first)	3D1	23 August 1847	18 June 1856	n/a
Strood (second)	3D1	30 July 1849	Open	16 August 1971*
Strood	see Rochester Bridge; renamed Rochester Bridge 1 April 1861 and Rochester & Strood 1 November 1861			
Sturry	6C1	1 June 1847	Open	1 May 1862
Swale Halt (first)	4F2	November 1917	20 April 1960	n/a
Swale Halt (second)	4F2	20 April 1960	Open	n/a
Swanley Junction (first)	1D2	1 July 1862	16 April 1939	16 April 1939
Swanley Junction (2nd)	see Swanley; renamed unknown			
Swanley Junction	1D2	16 April 1939	Open	16 May 1964*
Swanscombe (Blue Circle)	2B5	Unknown	n/a	1981
Swanscombe (first)	2B5	2 November 1908	6 July 1930	n/a
Swanscombe (second)	2B5	6 July 1930	Open	n/a
Swanscombe Halt	see Swanscombe, suffix dropped 5 May 1969			
Tankerton Halt	6A3	July 1914	1 January 1931	n/a
Tenterden	see Rolvenden; renamed 16 March 1903			
Tenterden St Michaels	13F4	1912	4 January 1954	n/a
Tenterden Town**	13G3	16 March 1903	4 January 1954	12 June 1961
Teston Crossing Halt	11C2	1 September 1909	2 November 1959	n/a
Thames Steels	4D3	Unknown	n/a	Open
Thamesport	4D4	Unknown	n/a	Open
The Dyke	30G5	1 September 1887	1 January 1939	2 January 1933
The Pilot	25F1	24 May 1928	November 1983	n/a
The Pilot Halt	see The Pilot; renamed 1947			
Three Bridges	19C2	12 July 1841	Open	4 May 1964
Three Oaks & Guestling (Halt)	see Three Oaks; renamed 1980			
Three Oaks	34C3	1 July 1907	Open	n/a
Three Oaks Bridge	see Three Oaks; renamed Three Oaks & Guestling Halt			

KENT AND SUSSEX

Station	Map ref	Opened	Closed (passengers)	Closed (freight)
Ticehurst Road	see Stonegate; renamed 16 June 1947			
Tilmanstone Colliery	16A2	May 1913	n/a	31 December 1987
Tilmanstone Colliery Halt	16A2	By August 1921	By July 1930	n/a
Tivoli, Margate	8B2	1 December 1846	c1872	n/a
Tonbridge	10F4	1864	Open	31 October 1986
Tonbridge Junction	see Tonbridge; renamed July 1929			
Tovil	11C3	1883/4	15 March 1943	n/a
Tovil Goods	11C3	1883/84	n/a	3 October 1977
Tunbridge Junction (first)	10F4	26 May 1842	1864	n/a
Tunbridge Junction (second)	see Tonbridge; renamed Tonbridge Junction May 1893			
Tunbridge	see Tunbridge Junction (first); renamed January 1852			
Tunbridge Wells (first)	21B1	25 November 1846	1 September 1851	Unknown
Tunbridge Wells (second)	21B1	1 September 1851	Open	n/a
Tunbridge Wells Central	see Tunbridge Wells (second); suffix carried 9 July 1923 to 1986			
Tunbridge Wells	see Tunbridge Wells West; name changed 22 August 1923			
Tunbridge Wells West	21B1	1 October 1866	8 July 1985	4 September 1961
Tyler Hill	6C3	3 May 1830	1846	n/a
Tyler Hill Halt	see Blean & Tyler Hill Halt; known as Tyler Hill Halt May 1912 to December 1915			
Uckfield (first)	31E4	18 October 1858	13 May 1991	5 August 1968
Uckfield (second)	31E4	13 May 1991	Open	n/a
Upnor	3C3	1875	31 December 1961	31 December 1961
Uralite Halt	2B1	July 1906	4 December 1961	n/a
Wadhurst	22E2	1 September 1851	Open	3 September 1962
Waldron & Horam Road	see Horam; renamed Waldron & Horam 1 January 1935			
Waldron & Horam	see Horam; renamed 21 September 1953			
Walmer	17C3	15 June 1881	Open	2 October 1961
Warnham	18D4	1 May 1867	Open	5 April 1965*
Warnham Brick Works	18D2	Unknown	n/a	Unknown
Warren Bridge Halt	25C2	16 July 1927	1927	n/a
Warren Halt	see Warren Bridge Halt; renamed 1927			
Wateringbury	11D1	25 September 1844	Open	4 September 1961
West Bexhill Halt	see Collington; renamed Collington Halt November 1929			
West Brighton	see Hove (second); renamed Hove & West Brighton 1 October 1894			
West Grinstead	29B3	16 September 1861	7 March 1966	7 May 1962
West Hoathly**	20E2	1 August 1882	17 March 1958	13 June 1955
West Malling	11B1	1 June 1874	Open	16 May 1964
West St Leonards	34E5	1887	Open	n/a
West Worthing	38C5	4 November 1889	Open	n/a
Westenhanger & Hythe	see Westenhanger; renamed 1 October 1874			
Westenhanger	15D3	7 February 1844	Open	25 March 1963
Westenhanger Racecourse	15D3	Unknown	Mid-1960s	n/a
Westerham	9C2	7 July 1881	30 October 1961	30 October 1961
Westgate-on-Sea	8B4	April 1871	Open	6 November 1961
Westham & Pevensey	see Pevensey & Westham; renamed January 1851			
Whitstable (LCD)	see Whitstable Town (first); renamed Whitstable-on-Sea July 1879			
Whitstable & Tankerton	see Whitstable; renamed 1979			
Whitstable (CW)	6A4	4 May 1830	March 1846	n/a
Whitstable (second)	6A4	February 1894	1 January 1931	1 March 1953
Whitstable	6A4	1 January 1915	Open	18 April 1964
Whitstable Harbour	6A4	19 March 1932	n/a	1 March 1953
Whitstable Town (first)	6A4	1 August 1860	1 January 1915	n/a
Whitstable Town (second)	see Whitstable; renamed Whitstable & Tankerton 1 February 1936			
Whitstable (first)	6A4	March 1846	February 1894	n/a
Whitstable-on-Sea	see Whitstable Town (first); renamed 1 July 1899			
Willingdon	41C4	see Hampden Park; renamed Hampden Park for Willingdon 1 July 1903		
Winchelsea	24F2/34A1	13 February 1851	Open	1 May 1961
Winchelsea Halt	see Winchelsea; 'Halt' suffix used 12 June 1961 to 5 May 1969			
Wingham Colliery	1A5	Unopened	n/a	Unopened
Wingham Colliery Halt	7E3	1916	1 November 1948	n/a
Wingham Town	7E2	1925	1 November 1948	n/a
Wingham, Canterbury Road	7E2	1925	1 November 1948	1 March 1951
Witherenden	see Stonegate; renamed Ticehurst Road December 1851			
Withyham	21C4	2 January 1967	6 November 1961	
Wittersham Road**	24B1	2 February 1900	4 January 1954	12 June 1961
Wivelsfield	30C3	1 August 1886	Open	n/a
Woodgate	36B3	8 June 1846	1 June 1864	unknown
Woodnesborough	7E5	1925	1 November 1948	1 March 1951
Woodnesborough Colliery	see Woodnesborough; renamed July 1931			
Worthing (first)	38C5	24 November 1845	1869	n/a
Worthing (second)	38C5	1869	Open	11 May 1970
Worthing Central	see Worthing (second); suffix 'Central' added 5 July 1936 to 4 March 1967			
Wrotham & Borough Green	see Borough Green & Wrotham; renamed 18 June 1962			
Wye	14A1	6 February 1846	Open	10 June 1963
Yalding	11E1	25 September 1844	Open	27 May 1963
Yantlet Test Station	4C5	Unknown	n/a	Unknown
Yapton	36B1	8 June 1846	1 June 1864	n/a

*	Closed for all goods traffic except private sidings; these closed later.
**	Station now preserved.
***	Train service withdrawn 24 February 1969 and replaced by bus service; this was withdrawn on 4 May 1969 and station closed.
****	This halt was possibly never actually used.
*****	Had a variety of names prior to closure; reopened 1977 solely for school traffic.
+	No separate freight facilities; handled parcels traffic until date quoted.
++	Platforms still extant as unsigned staff halt.
+++	Temporary closure; permanently closed 1951/52 but used thereafter for excursion trains; now an unadvertised staff halt.